Easing the Burden of Stigma

Easing the Burden of Stigma

EASING THE BURDEN OF STIGMA

Stigma-informed Care and Support Interventions

Yvon Dandurand
Amy Davies
Chrystal Lattie

DCA - Legend

ISBN: 978-1-7383584-3-4

© 2025 Yvon Dandurand, Amy Davies and Chrystal Lattie
All rights reserved. No part of this book may be reproduced in any manner whatsoever without written permission except in the case of brief quotations embodied in critical articles and reviews.
First Printing, 2025

Acknowledgments

The authors wish to thank all study participants for their willingness to candidly share with them their experience of coping with stigma. They wish to thank Ms. Sofia Porta who helped with the research. They are also grateful for the valued assistance they received from colleagues at Elizabeth Fry Society of Greater Vancouver (EFry), Archway Community Services, and Connective Support Society.

This project was made possible by the support and funding of Women and Gender Equity Canada for which the authors are also very grateful.

CONTENTS

1 Introduction 1
2 The Burden of Stigma 5
3 The Sticky Stigma of a Criminal Conviction 23
4 Spoiled Identities and Related Hardship 39
5 Gender and Stigma 59
6 Coping with Stigma 79
7 A Stigma-informed Approach 111
8 Conclusion 127

REFERENCES 129
TERMS AND DEFINITIONS 155

1

Introduction

Erving Goffman defined stigma as "the situation of the person who is disqualified from full social acceptance" (Goffman, 1963: preface). One may be able to function socially without full social acceptance but, as they say, it gets complicated and sometimes extremely difficult.

The manipulation of social intolerance by power seeking individuals is not new, but its 21st century manifestation through social media is. A social stigma is an expression of a group's intolerance. Throughout the ages, social intolerance has been guided, focused and directed by various secular, moral or religious authorities to affirm their power and pursue their own objectives.

In many ways, the social intolerance expressed through various stigmas has also served to build and consolidate group cohesion and improve cooperation. Through various processes members of a group or society develop collective clarity about what to tolerate and what to reject. Adopting and sharing a group's intolerance is a proven way to demonstrate one's belonging to that group and to seek that group's acceptance. Similarly, once individuals lose their certainty about what they ought to tolerate, they tend to also lose their certainty about what they need to do to be accepted or to belong. Their self-identity may even be affected.

It is perhaps more important than ever before to try to understand how social stigmas affect our life and the lives of those whom as professionals we are trying to help. We live in a context where cultural phenomena such as the cancel culture and identity politics exacerbate intolerance. One may see this as a form of dysregulated or dysfunctional intolerance, but it is hardly new. Various forms of collective intolerance and the associated shaming and stigmatization have existed for a long time, but they have obviously been magnified by social media platforms (Mueller, 2021).

The negative labels change over time. Sometimes, they are replaced by putatively less stigmatizing ones. A "delinquent" becomes a "young offender", and then a "justice involved youth". An incorrigible or wayward youth is a "youth at risk." A "victim" is no longer a "victim" but a "survivor." A "drug addict" becomes "someone who suffers from a substance use disorder." A "homeless person" is someone who is houseless or in a "situation of homelessness". These efforts to avoid using stigmatizing language are well meaning and, in the long term, may help raise public awareness. However, they barely disguise the fact that the new labels can still support the same stigmas.

The purpose of this book is to advance stigma-informed practices within organizations dedicated to helping individuals through difficult life circumstances and transitions. During our study, people in recovery, reintegrating the community after imprisonment, suffering from mental health, or facing homelessness told us about one big problem they had in common: the stigmas and discrimination they were facing or anticipating. Unfortunately, that problem was only marginally addressed, if at all, by the people and organizations who were offering them support during difficult life transitions.

As helping professionals, do we know how the people we are trying to help live with, struggle and cope with the multiple and sometimes interacting stigmas they face? Can we help them cope with, manage, or defeat those stigmas? How do we ensure that our own interventions do not perpetuate the cycle of stigmatization?

The overall goal of a stigma-informed practice is to develop gender-responsive and culturally appropriate support interventions that increase our clients' autonomy, self-efficacy, agency and resilience while providing them with opportunities to regain control over aspects of their lives affected by stigma.

For helping professionals, the approach implies a reflection and an awareness of their own adherence to various stereotypes and stigmas and how they affect their helping relationships. It follows that a comprehensive approach to stigma-informed care and support interventions is required at every organizational level. Broad organizational culture changes may be necessary, recognizing how every member of a helping organization who interacts with clients can play a critical role in building relationships of trust and respect with them and make them feel safe.

A stigma-informed approach to care and support interventions stems from the realization that various forms of stigmatization and ostracization affect the individuals and groups we purport to help. It is grounded in an understanding that exposure to various social stigmas can impact an individual's psychological and social development and wellbeing, mental health, access to opportunities, and willingness or ability to seek and receive help. The approach recognizes the signs and widespread impacts of stigma, especially when they are internalized by individuals and undermine their self-identity, self-confidence and agency. It prepares practitioners to support people facing various stigmas and to empower them to adopt healthier stigma coping strategies.

The approach also seeks to avoid further stigmatizing individuals or enabling unhealthy coping mechanisms. It prioritizes the physical, psychological and emotional safety of service users and staff. Finally, the approach seeks to address the barriers that people affected by stigma typically experience when accessing care and support services.

Stigma-informed interventions provide care and support in a manner that considers a person's history of stigmatization and the current impacts stigma has on their life. Unfortunately, the source of the stigma itself cannot always be addressed. The social stereotypes and attitudes behind them are not easily changed, but people experiencing stigma can make choices about how they cope with and respond to it. Stigma-informed interventions therefore aim to empower individuals to make the best choices they can and adopt coping strategies that are healthy and appropriate to their circumstances. In some instances, individuals may need help to confront and change some of their own ways of coping with stigma.

This book is based on research conducted as part of a larger project of the Elizabeth Fry Society of Greater Vancouver (EFry), with funding from Women and Gender Equality Canada. The project involved developing a training program and tools to support the implementation of a stigma-informed approach to support interventions. Some of the research was also conducted as part of previous evaluations of EFry programs to assist criminalized women and women in the sex economy.

The study consisted of an extensive review of the relevant research literature, as well as semi-structured, open-ended interviews with individuals who had received or were receiving services from one of EFry's many programs or from programs delivered by Archway Community Services (Abbotsford, BC) or Connective Support Society (Fraser Valley, BC). In total 41 interviews were conducted, 36 with adults and 5 with youth, as well as focus group discussions with 14 individuals from the same client base. In total, there were 33 female and 22 male participants. Their voices are important, and we are quoting at some length many of the observations and experiences they generously shared with us.

2

The Burden of Stigma

For many vulnerable people the burden of stigma is crushing, discouraging, paralyzing. In this chapter we consider the impacts of stigma on people's lives and their families, but first we try to bring some clarity to the terms and concepts we use.

We have already mentioned the widely accepted definition of *stigma* advanced by Erving Goffman (1963): "The situation of the person who is disqualified from full social acceptance." Goffman also offered the very useful concept of *spoiled identity* to explain how stigma is a process by which the reaction of others spoils a normal identity (Goffman, 1963).

In ancient Greece, the term stigma referred to bodily signs designed to expose something unusual and bad about someone's moral status. "The signs were cut or burnt into the body and advertised that the bearer was a slave, a criminal, or a traitor – a blemished person, ritually polluted, to be avoided, especially in public places" (Goffman, 1963: 1). Today, the term applies more to the disgrace itself rather than the physical evidence of it.

Stigmas are typically the result of negative attitudes towards a particular group (Cremin et al., 2021). These attitudes, which can be implicit or explicit, are comprised of beliefs, feelings, and behaviours (Engel & Sheppard, 2020; Huskin et al., 2018). The behaviours involve actions or an intention to act and can include discriminatory acts, ostracization, exclusion and even violence. Link and Phelan defined stigma as "the co-occurrence of its components – labeling, stereotyping, separation, status loss, and discrimination" and posited that for stigmatization to occur, power must be exercised (Link & Phelan, 2001: 363). Some researchers argue that "stigma itself is punitive in its effects" (Sharpe, 2024: 4).

Stigmatization does not occur only among strangers. Many of the people we met for this study related stories of rejection by or exclusion from their own family. For example, a woman returning to her family after a period of incarceration said:

> *"When I returned to my children, they did not look at me like I had hoped they would. I do not know what ideas people have put in their heads. They don't call me 'mum', they refuse to do it. I did not take that well. I always call my mother 'mum'. My children do not realize what I went through. They don't understand why I left them."*

Thanks to communication technology, we now live at a time when people face the possibility of *instant mass stigmatization*. Social media have exacerbated social intolerance through the power of public backlash. The call-out culture (or cancel culture) spreads a new form of terror, supporting a mob mentality that hides under the pretense of speaking the truth to power.

We heard the story of a fifteen-year-old girl who threatened to commit suicide. The mother had called the police and, once the situation was somewhat defused, the girl explained how she had accepted to testify in court against a teacher who had molested her. Her sports coach, who found out about her intention to testify, decided to "out" her and post that information on social media, together with well crafted insults. The girl felt so hurt by how her friends responded to that information and so much feared seeing them again at school that she had decided to kill herself.

The Experience of Stigma

An old man who had been released after a very long period of incarceration wondered:

> *"They told me that I was a free person. What does it mean to be free if everyone excludes you and you feel you are under constant surveillance because of your past? I don't know when I will be back to being considered a full human being again."*

A middle-aged woman who had experienced homelessness and hardship because of her spouse's poor financial decisions told us:

> *"A lot of people are prepared to assume all kinds of things about you once they have pegged you as a homeless, or addicted, or a mentally ill person. You can tell by their attitude and how it changes once they find out about your little secret, or sometimes not so secret problem. The minute people realized I was homeless, for example, they treated me differently. Also, people get it wrong. For example, it is not because you're homeless that you are necessarily a drug addict or an incompetent or unreliable person. I am tired of being treated like a druggy. I have never used in my life. I tell you: people don't understand what it's like to be homeless, they have no idea."*

Another woman who had experienced homelessness shared her experience of feeling blamed and stigmatized for a situation for which she bore no responsibility:

> *"I became homeless after having left my work and moved to help my sick mother. My mother passed away and I found myself with nothing at all, on the street, homeless. None of that was my fault, but people seem to insist on finding out and telling me where I went wrong."*

Other formerly homeless persons wanted us to know the following:

> *"You go to a place like Wendy's or Tim Hortons around here and they stop you at the door. Even if you have money and could be a paying customer, they don't want you around. Some of them won't sell food to you. They won't let you use their toilets. Often, they are very rude. I don't know why. I suppose that it is because people*

make a mess in the toilets or go and sleep there for three hours or use drugs in there. Or maybe, they are afraid, or they think that their clients may be afraid of you."

"If you go to … (a retail store), they often follow you around and stare at you. I want to ask them what's their problem. They sometimes want to search you or your bag even if no one saw you take anything at all. I don't let them; they have no business searching my things. Sometimes they kick me out (not literally). I get so sick of it."

We heard from youth who felt they were caught in some kind of culture-conflict situation where the only behaviour that was acceptable at home was precisely what exposed them to various forms of ostracization at school and among their friends. Some of them shared the following:

"In my own mind, I may be tempted sometimes to hide who I am, to get rid of some of the most obvious symbols of my belonging to a religion, but I don't because I know that it is important to protect the bloodline, including my religious bloodline. I don't think that I would ever do that."

"I am sometimes stigmatized or criticized because of my poor knowledge of my own community's language: 'You are old enough; you should have learned by now'. Because of that, people sometimes seem to question how religious I am, but they don't know how often I pray, or what is in my heart."

"My own community is very harsh with young women. My high school friends do not always understand why I have to do certain things. There is a strict code of conduct I must respect; everyone around me, including all the aunties enforce all kinds of rules. It gets even worse when the men get involved. They all seem to think that they are perfect, more religious, that they can dictate religious beliefs to others. Sometimes, they just make up this stuff. Religion is just used as a pretext for controlling us, especially girls."

"My school friends do not always understand what my community expects from me. For example, marrying out of our religion would be a big deal for me, but not necessarily for them. I feel that

they judge me sometimes for complying with the rules of my culture."

"I regret having defied the rules of my parents to please my school friends. Now I go forward, and I try not to cause trouble."

Some types of stigmatization are more present in certain locations, within certain groups, or even at certain times. One immigrant to Canada who had experienced extreme stigmatization, even violence and persecution, in one tight-knit rural community remarked:

"I am Mexican but have lived mostly in Canada since I was eight. Sometimes it makes no difference that I am an immigrant, but sometimes it does. I suppose it is a matter of where you end up going. Some places are quite bad."

Stigma is also related to place. Territorial stigma, as it is sometimes referred to, is about to the negative social judgment attached to people living, working or frequenting certain places (Wacquant, 2007). Some stigmas adhere to communities of place, like people who live on the wrong side of town. Territorial stigma affects identifiably disadvantaged places and the people who live there. It is also very instructive to note that, within an area labelled by outsiders as "bad", insiders sometimes project this reputation onto certain streets or groups of people as a way of disassociating themselves from an anticipated stigma (Meade, 2021).

Stigmatization is sometimes exercised among people who face the same stigmatizing situation. For example, a woman reminded us of the stigma attached to using crack, even among drug users. A transgender woman, in an addiction recovery program, told us:

"Many women in this program think that I should not even be here at all. They have many ways to let me know that, including one of them who was very insulting and abusive."

Another told us:

"It's funny, when I come here (a drop-in centre for women) women who are in recovery seem to resent me because I do not have an addiction problem. It is as if they are thinking that my problems

are not serious enough or that I am taking help that does not belong to me."

People often expressed a feeling of exhaustion because of constantly having to face and fight stigmatization and exclusion: "I feel exhausted", one of them confided, "(...) but what can I do? It's everywhere. What am I supposed to do? I can't just disappear to make everyone else feel more comfortable."

Different Types of Stigmas

The following are definitions of concepts that can help us understand the social dynamics of stigmatization and the different individual responses to it.

Public stigma refers to public attitudes, implicit or explicit, towards a stigmatized group, or how the public or a community views a stigmatized group (Corrigan & Watson, 2002). Public stigmas take many forms and some of them are more disabling than others.

Enacted stigma is a manifestation of public stigma through actions, inactions and intentions to act targeting the stigmatized group.

Perceived stigma refers to people's perception that they or others like them are being stigmatized.

Anticipated stigma refers to an expectation or fear of experiencing enacted stigma. Such expectations can be debilitating, leading to isolation, social disengagement and an inability to seize various opportunities or to seek assistance (Scambler, 1998; Fox, Smith & Vogt, 2016; Moore, Stuewig & Tangney, 2016; Luoma, 2011; Rayson & Alba, 2019; Yip et al., 2023).

Self-stigma (internalized stigma) refers to situations where someone identifies with a stigmatized group, accepts the negative judgment of others, and internalizes negative thoughts, feelings, and self-evaluations associated with the stigmatized identity (Corrigan, Watson, & Barr, 2006; Luoma et al., 2007). It is, as will be discussed in more details, a major source of psychological stress.

Intersectional stigma (compounded stigma) refers to the convergence of multiple stigmatized identities within a person or group, and the resulting need to address their joint or compounded effects on health and wellbeing.

Associative stigma (stigma by association) refers to the process whereby a person experiences stigmatization because of an association with a stigmatized person or group (Östman & Kjellin, 2002; Pryor, Reeder & Monroe, 2012). The term *courtesy stigma* is also used, for example, to refer to situations where the repercussions of stigma extend to families and addiction treatment professionals (Luoma, 2011).

Conspicuous versus concealable stigma. Some stigmas are associated with signs or characteristics that are apparent, but others are not – for example, race and gender as compared to mental health or addiction (Deakin, Fox & Matos, 2020; Moran, 2012).

Perceived and Anticipated Stigma

Researchers have developed tools to measure perceived stigmatization among people with a non-concealable stigma; for example, the Perceived Stigmatization Questionnaire (PSQ) and the Social Comfort Questionnaire (SCQ) (Lawrence et al., 2006). That has made it possible to conduct studies that compare perceived stigma with other behavioural patterns.

During our study, a few individuals mentioned that they had no idea whether a particular social stigma that they fit had had any real impact on their life. One person, for example, revealed:

"I am not sure that my criminal record has prevented anything, but I suspect that it has. Recently I had a job interview with the foodbank. While I could get a vulnerable sector clearance, I suspect that my record was one of the things that made them not pick me for the position. No one told me that it was a factor in their decision. I had to check the box on the application. I don't know for a fact that it was a factor. One never knows."

A woman remarked:

> "I don't always know why they avoid me or reject me. I don't think that people stigmatize me because I am Indigenous. People often try to make you feel like you don't belong, but you don't always know why."

A young woman had no idea whether people were treating her differently because of her criminal record:

> "My criminal record did not matter to me. It did not really affect my life or if it did, I did not know about it."

Indeed, many of the people we talked to mentioned that, in their own experience, one never knows for sure why people are distrusting you, stigmatizing you, excluding you.

> "They don't necessary tell you to your face that they don't trust you. They don't tell you why either."

> "They don't always tell you the truth, they invent bogus reasons for distrusting you or avoiding you, maybe to give themselves a good conscience."

> "I can be a bit paranoid, but I am not crazy. I know when people are scheming behind my back."

Another woman confided:

> "When my husband killed himself, I got blamed for that and I guess I blamed myself as well, but it had nothing to do with me. People, I guess, always need to find someone to blame. Sometimes it is convenient for them to blame you. That way they don't have to look at themselves."

One woman talked to us about the pain associated with becoming aware of how stigma was affecting her:

> "When you get sober, it is scary, you become aware of what was going on around you, what people are doing to you and what they think of you. People's reaction made me feel alone, scared, like my whole life was not real, like an illusion. That's really scary. To realize now how people were treating me and lying to me and knowing that I was not even aware of that is part of my motivation to get

treatment and deal with my addiction issues. It is like I have been living in a different reality. Now, I process things differently. I did not pick up on things that people were doing. Now I am more aware of all that."

Anticipated Stigma

Anticipated stigma is linked to the fear of the judgment of others. One woman in her early sixties with a persistent substance use problem, shared how she was affected by the judgment of others, especially in relation to her addiction:

"The judgment of others is one of my triggers. If people think the worst about me, so what's the difference. You may as well do it. If people are not going to change their view, what's the point. But today, I know that I should not, cannot, care about that. (...) Honestly, I still feel a lot of shame. I am still worried about how people look at me, what they are saying about me behind my back. Maybe it is all in my head, but I don't know what they are really thinking."

The fear of being stigmatized or even "canceled" by other youth was very present in the high school age youth we talked with. They were worried and very vigilant. They took great care to avoid behaviour, words, signs that could bring about some kind of stigmatization. One of them, betraying some exasperation, said

"I wish it was easier to express my views without fear of judgement or consequences. I feel it is important to become my own person and that I have to learn by myself, but that is not encouraged."

Another one added:

"When you are faced with the constant negative judgement of others, it sets you back. It affects your self-confidence. It makes you sad. It holds you back also. It is harder to dare to be yourself."

During the study, we heard from people who claimed to have developed a kind of special vigilance, an ability to recognize individuals who are likely to enact stigmas and to anticipate problematic situations. One of them explained:

> *"It takes three to five seconds to find out whether someone is going to judge you or treat you with some respect. It is easy to read the signs, the body language. (...) One of these signs is when people are trying to avoid contact with you."*

She added that one can take some protective steps when anticipating stigma: "If people avoid you, you just avoid them back."

One young woman said:

> *"The fear of stigma does not help you as you're developing your own identity. I tell my friends who are struggling that they should really believe in themselves: "Don't change who you are just because you are afraid of what other kids may say or think. Be proud of who you are and where you come from."*

The anticipation of stigma is also very present among people with a criminal record who are seeking employment. The following are some examples:

> *"When I know that my criminal record is likely to come up, I am discouraged to apply, especially for the job I would actually like, like working for the BC Ferries. (...) I thought of applying to the navy. I signed up for the aptitude test, but I am not sure how open they are about accepting someone with a criminal record."*

> *"When they (employers) ask, it is so embarrassing. One time, I had been working on and off as a cook for an employer that had several operations, including and addiction centre. When the employer sold the business to another company, we were all asked for a criminal record check. Once mine came back it prevented me from working in that centre."*

> *"It was so long ago and so minor, but it still follows me. When employers find out about your record, none of it is ever played to you. You just find out about their decision. (...) It is humiliating."*

Concealable Stigma

Some stigmas are more concealable than others. Individuals with concealable stigmatized identities possess characteristics, such as alcoholism, that are not apparent in the way that skin colour or other visible characteristics are, yet if revealed could cause a loss of social status (Koken, 2012). These individuals may not possess any obviously devalued attributes but are nevertheless struggling with enacted and anticipated stigmas and their related consequences (Tally & Littlefield, 2014). We will see, in Chapter 5, how they engage in various information control strategies to conceal or selectively disclose information about their situation.

Self-stigma

Self-stigma occurs when affected individuals "endorse and apply the negative public stereotypes associated with their condition to themselves, leading to diminished self-esteem" (Hing & Russel, 2017: 417). Higher levels of self-stigma are often associated with greater secrecy and withdrawal (Hing & Russel, 2017). Yet, secrecy can be very damaging because it impedes problem acknowledgment, recovery, and help-seeking. It also creates heightened anxiety and stress through the vigilance and efforts needed to keep a spoiled identity hidden (Corrigan, Kosyluk & Rüsch, 2013; Hing & Russel, 2017).

Once internalized, stigma persists and reproduces the effects of the externalized stigma (Sinko et al., 2020). Stigma internalizing is influenced by culture and context, as well as past experiences (Yu et al., 2021). Internalizing prejudice is not a necessary consequence of stigma (Corrigan & Rao, 2012). For example, people who endorse the stigma of mental illness do not always internalize it or suffer diminished-self-esteem and self-efficacy (Corrigan, Watson & Barr, 2006).

The internalization of stigma (self-stigma) is sometimes conceptualized (Corrigan & Rao, 2012) as a three-stage process:

(1) *Awareness* about the condition(s) and the associated negative stereotypes. This includes the negative feelings and emotional reactions the individual has towards their certain conditions.

(2) *Agreement* - the individual internalizes and agrees that these negative stigmatizing stereotypes about them are true.

(3) *Application* - the person agrees that the stereotypes apply to themselves, thereby negatively impacting their self-esteem.

For the stigmatized individual, the judgment of certain persons is of course more important than that of others. Some key people in one's life obviously matter more than others. For example, for a Catholic the judgment and behaviour of a priest may be especially important. That can have an impact on whether a stigma is internalized.

A young man explained:

> *"Generally, I have not experienced a lot of negativities from people around me. To be honest, I found a lot of people were prepared to accept the new me. Out there, there are people who are willing to help you. Inside me, it's a different story. I have had to learn to trust myself and to trust people."*

Very few of the people we met during the study readily admitted having internalized the stigma that affected them, but their denial did not always sound very convincing. Others seem to be proud of their ability to brush off other people's judgment. A woman in her early thirties who had previously been involved in the sex industry proudly declared:

> *"It does not bother me anymore. I am so used to that. Everyday, there is someone who harasses me. I tell myself 'fuck it'."*

There is often a resistance to acknowledge self-stigma. It is rooted in identity, self-image, even local culture. We were often told that people need an opportunity, and a safe place, to talk about things they are not used to talk about, a place of acceptance where they can peel away the different layers of stigma and face them. But for many, facing a stigma once is only one discrete experience. Life goes on and the judgment of others continues to weigh heavily.

A woman who had complained to her employer about being sexually harassed by her supervisor (in a large public institution) found herself actively ostracized by most of her colleagues and her supervisor and was pressured to resign from her position. She explained how she fought hard to avoid internalizing the judgement of others and she shared the following:

> *"I felt like I was alone and that I was the only one in that kind of situation. Do you know how hard it is to feel like the whole world has turned against you? I felt isolated, but I also isolated myself. It is as if I needed time to grieve. (...) I most value my independence, without it I have become very vulnerable. I have felt vulnerable for a long time. I still do, maybe. I don't date. I have not had a relationship in about six years. I am still hoping. I think that I am an optimistic person."*

She later added:

> *"Facing stigma, in a sense, was an opportunity for in-depth self-discovery. I guess you could say I embarked on a journey of self-improvement. I learned a lot. On the positive side, the whole negative experience taught me how to be self-reliant and I became very resourceful. I am now in a place where I no longer care about what people think of me. I am oozing self-confidence, but I experienced a lot of self-doubt over the years; I came back."*

Several people told us about the need to guard against internalizing social stigma. One of them talked about the need to think positively. Another offered the following advice:

> *"Stigma can be self-destructive if you let it. You have to be preventive. Seek the help. Don't let it get to you."*

Someone made the following suggestion about how to fight off stigma and avoid internalizing it:

> *"The best way to deal with that is to remind yourself that we all make mistakes and that you are doing what you can to improve. Don't let people's judgment drag you down and keep you down. (...)*

Shame on them for being like that. But don't show anger or disrespect. Don't let that get the best of you."

Self-stigma can easily cut people off from the support they need. However, for various reasons, the expected negative reaction from family members and others sometimes does not materialize. One person with a mental health problem revealed:

. One person with a mental health problem revealed:

"My family is supporting me, being around me. I have a lot of people in my family that can help me. Before today, I did not want their help. I realize now that I was pushing them away and somehow told myself that they were rejecting me."

A woman victim of intimate partner violence explained:

"I had to get over this 'poor victim thing', the mental attitude, the victim mentality. I did not get help with that, but I worked at it. I told myself there are a lot of other victims and I thought 'what made me think that I could not be one of them, what made me so special?'. It made it worse for me that the police did not take me seriously because my partner was also in law enforcement. (...) Even at work, I felt I was a victim of negative judgment because I had been a victim of violence. I had a hard time accepting the injustice of it all. I could not swallow it. After all that time, I think that I am getting over it, but it is still very hard."

As will be seen later in more details, the most commonly reported correlates of the self-stigma are lower self-esteem, higher depression, and higher symptom severity. Self-esteem was found in numerous studies to be the strongest predictor of self-stigma. For example. internalized weight stigmas appear to be associated with higher levels of body image concern, anti-fat attitudes, depressive symptoms and stress, and with lower levels of self-esteem (Durso, Latner & Ciao, 2016). Similarly, the self-stigma related to problem gambling, like the stigma attached to other mental health disorders, has a negative impact on self-esteem and coping (Hing & Russel, 2017). Higher levels of self-stigma related to gambling were found to be associated with being female, being older, having lower self-esteem, higher problem gambling severity score and greater use of secrecy and withdrawal (Hing & Russel, 2017). Very importantly, in such instances, self-stigma negatively predicts decisions to seek both mental health and counseling information (Lannin et al., 2016).

The shame associated with self-stigma correlates with poor self-esteem, negative self-concept, and multiple mental health issues. Research also suggests that experiencing high levels of shame increases the risk for a range of high-risk behaviours, including substance use, self-harm, and suicidal ideation (Tilghman-Osborne et al., 2008). Stigma, like trauma, can trigger some self-defeating and self-destructive behaviours. For example, individuals with concealable stigmatized identities are at an increased risk for problematic substance use (Tally & Littlefield, 2014; Martin et al., 2020).

Corrigan, Watson and Barr (2006) examined self-stigma at three levels: stereotype agreement, self-concurrence, and self-esteem decrement. They observed that people must first agree with a stigma before applying it to themselves. They also noted that stereotype agreement was strongly correlated with self-concurrence and a decrease in self-esteem (Corrigan, Watson & Barr, 2006).

Tools have been developed to measure the extent to which a mental illness stigma is internalized. For example, the Internalized Stigma of Mental Illness (ISMI) scale is a 29-item questionnaire that measures self-stigma among persons with psychiatric disorders. A review of 55 known versions of the ISMI scale found the scale reliable and valid for use across a wide range of settings, disorders, and cultures (Boyd et al., 2014; 2016).

Detrimental Impacts of Stigma

Studies have revealed that perceived and anticipated stigmas can have a direct impact on both psychological distress and physical health somatic symptoms (O'Donnell, Corrigan & Gallagher, 2015). Stigma is a fundamental determinant of behaviour, wellbeing and health for many marginalized groups. Several studies have found a strong correlation between internalized stigma and elevated depression levels, diminished self-esteem, and heightened symptom severity (Boyd et al., 2014).

Link & Phelan (2001) explained that, because of its pervasiveness, "stigma has a corrosive impact on the health of many and probably has a dramatic bearing on the distribution of life chances in such areas as earnings, housing, criminal involvement, health, and life itself" (Link & Phelan, 2001: 363; also, Hatzenbuehler, Phelan & Link, 2013). Several studies have found a strong correlation between internalized stigma and elevated depression levels, diminished self-esteem, and heightened symptom severity (Boyd et al., 2014).

People with a keen consciousness of stigma tend to perceive more discrimination than those with a lower level of stigma consciousness (Bos et al., 2013). Studies have also shown that group identification and feeling a common bound with fellow members of disadvantaged or marginalized group is strongly related to perceptions of both personal and group stigma (LeBel, 2012).

People struggling with various stigmas often report feeling dehumanized. Interpersonal dehumanizing behaviours are observed across various types of interpersonal relationships, including close relationships with family members and friends, and in other relational contexts, such as in the workplace, medical settings, or sporting contexts (Karantzas, Simpson & Haslam, 2023).

Microaggressions are sometimes experienced by persons suffering from a mental illness or substance addiction (Gonzales et al., 2015). Since the intentions behind that kind of behaviour are not necessarily declared, stigmatized individuals do not always know how to interpret the behaviour and are sometimes puzzled by what is triggering such an abusive reaction.

Another less obvious but nevertheless serious ways in which stigmatized individuals are affected is when others around them, including people purporting to help them, are withholding sympathy or empathy.

For example, patients who continue to smoke after a cancer diagnosis apparently encounter negative reactions and little empathy, and the related stigma may negatively impact health outcomes (Luberto et al., 2016).

There is incontrovertible evidence that the experience of both subtle and blatant forms of stigma impedes access to treatment and recovery and generates psychological and physical health disparities (Bos et al., 2013; Judd et al., 2023; Fang et al., 2021; Luoma et al., 2007; Luoma, 2011; Himmelstein, Puhl & Quinn, 2017; Fox, Smith & Vogt, 2018). Self-stigma and anticipated stigma often lead to withdrawal, isolation, social distancing, and what some have referred to as "disengaged living", and therefore poor quality of life (Yip et al., 2023). In a study of veterans with symptoms of depression, anticipated stigma was found directly related to increased absenteeism and decreased work functioning (Fox, Smith & Vogt, 2016).

Additionally, anticipated stigma is known to be one reason for youth's non-participation in various crime prevention and mental health programs designed for them, including sports-based programs (Dandurand & Heidt, 2023; Appelqvist-Schmidlechner, Haavalammi & Kekonen, 2023). In fact, we also know that stigmatization often occurs because of poorly designed programs targeting vulnerable or "at risk" youth (Dandurand & Heidt, 2023; Chamberlain, 2013; Eckholm, 2019).

3

The Sticky Stigma of a Criminal Conviction

A criminalized lifestyle comes with significant social stigma, segregation and social exclusion. The stigma attached to a criminal conviction is ubiquitous, long lasting, and powerful. It can be transferred to a convicted individual's associates, relatives and children. It is based on public fears, some of them reasonable and others imagined or exaggerated. That mark is often indelible, and the stigma associated with it can be extremely hard to shed.

A criminal record can damage a person regardless of whether it relates to extensive or minor criminal justice contacts (Ispa-Landa & Loeffler, 2016). In fact, someone does not have to be convicted to experience the stigma. It is usually sufficient to be suspected or accused of a crime or, as the media often say, to be someone "known to the police." Being acquitted is not necessarily sufficient to put a stop to the stigma and repair a damaged reputation, neither is being officially exonerated after a wrongful conviction (Konvisser, 2015; Kuckuca, Applegarth & Mello, 2020; Kuckuca et al., 2021).

A sixty-one-year-old Metis woman told us about anticipated stigma and confirmed bias. She explained how, in her experience, the stigma attached to a criminal record often simply confirms other biases about Indigenous people:

"For me the stigma attached to my criminal record was mostly a source of embarrassment, but it also created problems with seeking

employment. Because I am Indigenous, that stigma built on top of the stigma and discrimination suffered by Indigenous people. (...) People think that it is no surprise that I have a criminal record since I am Indigenous. (...) All Indigenous people are familiar with that social bias. For example, I do not drink, I never did. When people offer me a drink and I tell them I don't drink, they try to be sympathetic and they ask, 'how long have you been in recovery?'. The fact that I don't drink confirms their bias about Indigenous people all being alcoholics. (...) They probably don't believe they are racists; they just accepted the stereotype."

Public disclosure of criminal records amounts to a perpetual stigmatization (Corda, 2016). A criminal record has been shown to impact the health and quality of life of ex-offenders and hinder their access to health care services (Redmond et al., 2020; McWilliams & Hunter, 2021; McWilliams, Stidham & Hunter, 2022; Rima et al., 2022). Perceived discrimination by healthcare providers due to patients' criminal record is associated with significantly higher odds of fair to poor self-reported general health status (Redmond et al., 2020; Sundaresh et al., 2020).

The stigmatization of ex-prisoners represents a major obstacle to their successful rehabilitation and social reintegration (Moran, 2012). It affects their access to credit or financial services (Finlay, Mueller-Smith & Street, 2023), their ability to travel abroad, obtain a visa or acquire permanent residency (Blitsa et al., 2015), or the likelihood that they will be admitted to college (Stewart & Uggen, 2020) or find employment. As will be seen in more detail, that stigma affects the three main preconditions to a successful social reintegration: finding employment, finding suitable accommodation, and repairing relationships (Chin & Dandurand, 2018). Moreover, the self-stigma attached to being formally labelled as a criminal by the authorities and treated as such by the community deeply affects an individual self-identity and personality. It follows that addressing that psychological impact is also part to varying degrees of the offender rehabilitation and social reintegration project.

Professionals working in the field of social reintegration of offenders (both in prisons and in the community) are very aware of the social stigmatization and discrimination that many of their clients are facing (e.g., stigmas associated with criminal conviction, sex work, mental illness, or drug addiction). However, they may not always fully appreciate the debilitating impacts of stigma and the associated fears, guilt and self-deprecation. For instance, ex-offenders' non-disclosure or selective disclosure of their status, or their vigilance and self-isolation can easily be mistaken for an unwillingness to engage in a program instead of a normal self-protection reaction that affords them a degree of control over how they respond to stigma in their public and personal worlds.

This chapter is focused on the criminal stigma, in part because helping women reintegrate into society and reunite with their families after a criminal conviction is central to EFry's mission and mandate, but also because that stigma is one of the most difficult ones an individual may ever have to face. We had the opportunity to interview many individuals who had applied or were in the process of applying for a criminal record suspension once they had become eligible, several years after their latest conviction. They predictably had a lot to say about the impacts of a criminal record as a constant reaffirmation of their initial stigmatization.

Repairing Relationships

Criminalized individuals, especially after a period of incarceration, risk social isolation. Various studies indicate that an anticipated stigma during incarceration predict social withdrawal post-release (Moore, Stuewig & Tangney, 2013; 2016; Moore & Tangney, 2017).

Researchers have attempted to measure the impacts of a criminal record on online dating and found that the former had an impact on people's willingness to meet, socialize with or date a person with that stigma (Evans & Blount-Hill, 2022). However, the stigma did not have to same effect for all. A study of female online dating, involving women under parole supervision, revealed that the disclosure of that stigmatized status resulted in a significant reduction in the number of matches, and that the stigma of a criminal record was more damaging for Black and Latino females in comparison to White females (Evans, 2019; Evans & Blount-Hill, 2022).

For female offenders, desistance from crime and social reintegration are often linked to relational support networks and their identity as a mother, daughter, sister and friend. More so than for men, issues around criminalized women's relationships directly affect their likelihood of reoffending. It is sometimes argued that relationships are "women's most prevalent criminogenic need" (Farmer, 2019: 7). Unfortunately, criminalized women often experience a lack of strong, positive relational connections, making them vulnerable to abuse, victimization and dysfunctional relationships (Booth, Masson & Baldwin, 2018). This is partly why several studies have identified support from parole supervisors, service providers, and others as critical for increasing women's self-esteem and helping them to overcome social reintegration challenges (Stone et al., 2018).

Affirming a New Identity.

Criminalized individuals often struggle to distance themselves from their spoiled identity and to affirm a new one. According to a narrative identity theory of desistance, offenders who successfully desist from criminal activity have developed redemptive personal narratives that interpret past failures and traumatic experiences as necessary precursors to current and future success. Researchers have examined the role of the narrative construction of identity in desistance from criminal offending and substance use. They highlighted the fact that desistance processes can be construed as largely relational, involving the acceptance and recognition of desistance by others (Nugent & Schinkel 2016; Stone et al., 2018; Gâlnander, 2020). In other words, identities are dependent on other people's reactions and acknowledgment. One study found that desisting women often constructed narrative identities that emphasized their moral agency and resisted the stigmatizing discourse surrounding substance-using mothers (Stone, 2016).

Indeed, one can hardly overemphasize the importance of the relational aspects of desistance and social reintegration. As Gâlnander suggested:

> "Given that personal identity is dependent on social identity, individual reform in desistance processes can be conceptualized as being about making sense of one's past through recognition of change by others" (Gâlnander, 2020: 1302).

However, obtaining acceptance and recognition for such a change in lifestyle and disposition can prove difficult. A former prisoner talked to us about his participation in rehabilitation programs and his expectation that people around him would acknowledge that he had changed:

> *"It is nice to see people recognize that you have tried to change, that you are a different person. It is rare. (...) I am not sure what I can do to convince people around me that I have changed. I am a different man now, but people don't see that."*

Another former prisoner related a similar experience:

> *"People have a hard time believing that you have changed. They think offenders never change. I can understand that. In prison, you see people around you who come back after committing more crimes. You thought that they had changed. What were they thinking? (...) To be honest, I have been like that a few times in my life."*

Finding Employment

A criminal record is a significant barrier to employment, particularly employment that offers a decent wage, since employers generally interpret it as an indicator of spoiled identity (van den Berg et al., 2020; Rovira, 2024; Sheppard & Ricciardelli, 2020). Arrest, conviction and incarceration reduce odds of job search, decrease the number of search methods job seekers deploy, and direct job seekers away from search methods that are more efficient and effective at yielding offers (Smith & Broege, 2020). A criminal record acts as a "negative credential" that causes exclusion from the labour market and the reproduction of inequality among minority groups (Durnescu, 2021).

Female ex-offenders, who are often their children's primary caregiver, find it hard to find work and earn wages to support them. Male ex-offenders experience difficulties obtaining and retaining jobs that provide a living wage and allow them to afford child-support. In some instances, they may experience harsh child support enforcement remedies that further impairs their ability to obtain a job (Brito & Wood, 2023).

A study conducted for Public Safety Canada found that individuals released from federal institutions participated in the labour market less, made substantially less employment income, received more social assistance payments and filed taxes less often than the general Canadian population. Only half of the ex-prisoners surveyed indicated having found employment after 4 years with an average reported income of $14,000. Additionally, the study found that the barriers to employment following incarceration disproportionately affected women, Indigenous, and older individuals (Babchishin, Keown & Mularczyk, 2021).

The ex-prisoners we met for our study thought that it had become harder than ever before to get a decent job with a criminal record. Employers, they believed, were less tolerant and had new ways to find out whether someone has a record:

> *"I have worked in assisted care living programs for more than ten years, but because of my criminal record I cannot get this kind of job anymore."*
>
> *"The stigma attached to a criminal record mostly affected my employment. (...) For the most part, I am not asked about my criminal record, but that is changing. Recently employers seem to ask more often. Some restaurants ask for a criminal record check for a dish washer or a prep cook."*
>
> *"Walmart offered me a job. They withdrew their offer when they found out about my criminal record."*

> *"Now, years later, I am in social services and the criminal record is an obstacle. I think that it is even harder for women than men in that kind of situation."*

Some of the people we consulted hoped that a criminal record suspension (a pardon) would make a difference in their life, including mitigate the stigma associated with a criminal conviction. For example, a woman shared her hope with us:

> *"Having a criminal record made a huge difference in my life. Getting a pardon will make a big difference. It will close the door on my past and give me a chance to work and not worry about my record stopping me. I have not been able to work for many years."*

Many if not most ex-offenders ascribe positive value to work although they recognize that having a criminal record makes it harder to find a job. Many of them demonstrate a high level of job self-efficacy and have a positive mindset about work (Lucken & Brancale, 2023). However, ex-prisoners often lack self-presentation skills (or a lack of what Goffman referred to as a "personal front") which, in combination with learned helplessness, makes it more difficult for them to find employment. Some of them anticipate rejection and, as a result, experience frustration, anxiety, low self-confidence and discouragement. They may develop a "why try" attitude and stop looking for work.

This may explain why individuals with criminal records are more likely than their non-justice involved counterparts to rely primarily on self-employment (Finlay, Mueller-Smith & Street, 2023), or focus on participating in the underground economy where they can earn respect on their own terms (Durnescu, 2021).

Exclusions from Occupational Licensing Schemes

Numerous licensing schemes limit, as a public safety measure, the participation of certain individuals in sensitive types of activities or activities that may put them in contact with vulnerable people. These schemes often disqualify people with a criminal record or at least people with a certain type of criminal conviction. Disqualifying some individuals from participating in a sector or an industry can help protect the public and prevent criminal actors from accessing and criminalizing the industry. This has been done in many industries in Canada and across the world (e.g., taxi and vehicle for hire services, liquor sales, private security services, banking, maritime transport and container management, procurement services, etc.). For example, the *British Columbia Passenger Transportation Act* states that someone cannot drive a passenger directed vehicle if their criminal record includes a "prescribed matter" that is set out in the BC Passenger Transportation Regulation. Occupational licensing has an impact on both people with criminal records and those with pending charges. These disqualifications prevent people with a criminal records from pursuing the higher-paying jobs they strive for and often force them to settle for incomes substantially below the poverty line (Decker, 2021).

The Employers' Negative Attitudes

A growing percentage of employers are asking job applicants for a criminal record check. The practice is now generalized. The disclosed criminal record typically leads the employer to reject a job applicant, rescind a job offer, fire the employee or reassign them to a different, often less well paid, job.

Studies of employers' attitudes towards ex-offenders found persistent negative attitudes towards them. A Canadian study by Cook and her colleagues (2024) found that more than half of surveyed employers were requiring criminal background checks, and more than half described individuals with a criminal record as a greater risk or liability than those without. Twenty-two percent of them described ex-offenders as "dangerous", over half (fifty-one percent) of them would not hire a candidate with a criminal record (Cook et al., 2024: 23).

Other studies have tried to understand employers' attitudes and the conditions under which they could be more favourable to employing ex-offenders. A survey of California employers found that only 26 percent of them would seriously consider hiring an individual with a criminal record (Oselin et al., 2024). Several studies ("resume audit" studies) were conducted in which researcher submitted constructed resumes to prospective employers, randomly sending criminal record or non-criminal record versions of the resume to each job. This allowed researchers to measure the effect of a criminal record on callback rates, holding fixed all aspects of the application profile. Without fail, studies on the effect of a serious felony conviction (Pager, 2003; Pager, Bonikowski & Western, 2009; Batastini et al., 2017; Agan & Starr, 2018; Cerda-Jara, Elster & Harding, 2020; Leasure & Kaminski, 2021) and studies on the effect of arrests on less serious charges that did not result in a conviction (Uggen et al., 2014) found that employers discriminated against applicants with a prior criminal justice system interaction.

A similar effect was observed with respect to the impact of a juvenile conviction record (Taylor & Spang, 2017). Most studies focused on relatively recent records, but it also appears that records of convictions as old as ten years still reduced employer callback rates (Leasure & Andersen, 2016). People with both psychiatric and criminal histories experienced greater stigma from employers (Batastini et al., 2017). The effect was even more pronounced for sexual offenders; they reported a perceived loss of autonomy and increased self-isolating behaviours resulting from their inability to secure employment (Tovey, Winder & Blagden, 2023).

When employers were asked about what might encourage them to hire ex-offenders, it appeared that a college degree could alleviate a criminal record stigma but was not sufficient to eliminate its effects (Cerda-Jara, Elster & Harding, 2020). In one study, recent college graduates with criminal records reported that job offers were often rescinded once the employer found out about their criminal record at the end of the hiring process (Cerda-Jara & Harding, 2024). Another study examined how employers and state occupational licensing officials (e.g., licences for armed security guards) used evidence of rehabilitation in hiring decisions when applicants had criminal records (Denver & Ewald, 2018). That study identified two key factors that influenced such assessments: the applicants' post-conviction trustworthiness and credible testimony (Denver & Ewald, 2018).

Credentials or program completion can help those with a criminal history improve their employment prospects (Leasure & Kaminski, 2021; Santos, Jaynes & Thomas, 2023). A survey of managers asking them to make hypothetical hiring decisions concluded that a criminal record carries a high employability cost, but that the cost could be superseded by specific credentials that signal an applicant's reliability (Santos, Jaynes & Thomas, 2023). Factors such as having at least one year of relevant experience, a high school or a college degree, or references from a former employer or a professor positively influenced those decisions (Santos, Jaynes & Thomas, 2023: 584).

The Disclosure Dilemma

Even in situations where a prospective employer does not explicitly ask whether someone has a criminal record or require a background check, jobseekers with a criminal record are in a real bind about whether to proactively disclose their record or refrain from doing so, with both options having the potential for negative outcomes. When people proactively volunteer that they have a record, that disclosure may very well lead to a rejection of their application, with no explanation given. When they do not disclose their criminal record, their past can still come back to haunt them if the employer eventually finds out about the record through other means.

In the absence of reliable access to criminal records through official channels, some employers rely on informal means (community ties) to access information about the character of job applicants (Baffour et al., 2023). In many instances, that information may be wrong or misleading. The job applicant who is being rejected may not even be aware that this information is being collected and may never find out that this is the real reason behind the rejection.

Ex-offenders often engage in selective disclosure of their criminal record to manage employers' impressions of them (Ricciardelli & Mooney, 2018). Many of them, having previously experienced discrimination once their record had been revealed, report not applying to jobs at employers that require a criminal background check (Cerda-Jara &

Harding, 2024). Yet, these jobs tend to be the higher paying ones; for example, larger companies are both more likely to require background checks and on average pay workers more (Cook et al., 2024; Bloom et al., 2018). Even ex-offenders with a college degree report tailoring their applications away from high-paying jobs that are likely to reject them for having a criminal record (Cerda-Jara & Harding, 2024). A criminal record obviously closes the door to many employment opportunities.

IBased on her study of women's management of the criminal record stigma, Anita Grace concluded:

> "Broadly speaking, women indicated they have three options when it comes to managing their criminal record with potential employers: they can tell the truth, lie, or try to avoid the question. For each woman, and in each negotiation, the stakes are high; disclosing a criminal record may mean that employer is unable or unwilling to offer the position. Not disclosing risks being found out and rejected, both for being a 'criminal' and for being dishonest." (Grace, 2022: 78)

Managing the Criminal Stigma

Ex-offenders find ways to manage the criminal stigma as they seek employment (Grace, 2022). They adopt various strategies in attempts to distance or distinguish their current self from the stigmatized past self, such as by articulating their attachment to a good "core self" and to prosocial roles, like that of a worker (Grace, 2022: 75). They may attempt "passing" by not disclosing discrediting information and by crafting personal narratives that conceal a criminal past and display positive information. They may try to keep their status a secret by avoiding or withdrawing from interactions in which disclosure may occur.

The concept of *signaling* is relevant here. Think for example of tattoos as social signs or signals that convey different meanings to different people. They convey different social information depending on how diverse groups and individuals perceive and interpret them. Similarly, one may think of what individuals with a spoiled identity do to signal respectability or belonging.

In both the pre-hire and post-offer hiring contexts, ex-offenders may use *reparative impression management* tactics – apology, justification, excuse – to mitigate employers' integrity concerns (Ali, Lyons & Ryan, 2017). That stigma management tactic is often successful and researchers have tried to identify the most effective reparative impression management tactics for ex-offender job seekers when disclosing a criminal record. A study by Gardner, Ali and Ryan (2023) was able to link specific tactics to employment outcomes. It confirmed that a key stigma management tactic involves ex-offenders signaling that they feel remorse for their past actions, although justifications and excuses tend to reduce the effect of the remorse perception. It appeared that judgments of remorse were linked to judgments of sincerity that may induce empathy for the individual, and to judgments of trustworthiness (Gardner, Ali & Ryan, 2023).

The previously quoted study of how job seeking women manage the criminal stigma revealed that the affirmation of a positive alternate identity was a key stigma management technique:

> The stigma management strategies described by women in this study included not only the hiding or disclosing strategies discussed above, but also the interconnected ways in which they at tempted to distinguish their current 'employable' identity from their past 'criminalized' one." (Grace 2022: 82)

Finding Housing

Finding suitable housing is central to the social reintegration of ex-offenders as they seek to establish themselves as law abiding and economically self-sufficient citizens and try to shed the stigmatized identity associated with past incarceration. The challenges they face in accessing housing "seem to hinder their ability to shed the stigmatized identities" (Keene, Smoyer & Blankenship, 2018: 799). These challenges are especially arduous for women seeking suitable housing for both themselves and their children, for example as a precondition to reunification with their children after a period of incarceration.

Schneider (2018: 923) refers to the "prison to homelessness pipeline." A criminal record, in interplay with other factors such as race, significantly diminishes housing opportunities (DeMarco, 2023; Evans, Blount-Hill & Cubellis, 2019; Evans & Porter, 2015; Evans, 2016; Hamovitch et al., 2023; Schneider, 2018; 2019).

A significant percentage of people who find themselves in a homeless situation are struggling with the criminal stigma, among other stigmas. For vulnerable people, incarceration raises the risk of future homelessness. In Canada, many people exiting prison, whether they were convicted of a criminal offence or not, do not have secure housing upon release, and around one-third of offenders in Canada are likely to not have a fixed address upon their release (Roebuck, 2008). Certain subgroups are disproportionately vulnerable to post-incarceration homelessness, such as people with poor literacy, severe mental illness, trauma related brain injury, or a substance use disorder (Novac et al., 2006).

Criminalized individuals encounter numerous barriers to housing arising from both structural and interpersonal forms of stigma. As observed by Keene, Smoyer and Blankenship (2018), that kind of exclusion is enacted by individuals and groups, but it is also the result of policies that consider a past criminal conviction as a legal and valid reason to deny housing. Formerly incarcerated people are required to reveal concealable histories, "turning aspects of their past into their present, and potentially activating stigma and discrimination" (Keene, Smoyer & Blankenship, 2018: 799).

Housing providers increasingly rely on criminal background checks to screen applicants in the rental housing market. They often perceive ex-offenders as low in competence and sociability and are therefore less willing to rent to them (Berry & Wiener, 2020). Researchers often use discriminatory audits to measure the impact of a criminal record on housing (DeMarco, 2023; Kukucka et al., 2021; Leasure, 2019). These studies show how housing providers disqualify tenants with a criminal record, even without information about the severity or timing of the offences. This effect is even stronger in gentrifying neighborhoods (De-Marco, 2023).

Researchers who posed as convicted felons inquired by phone from real estate agents about renting an apartment identified a range of responses from these real estate agents, including: overt rejection, deferral of rental decision to landlords, agent ambivalence, concerns about financial ability to pay rent, and concealing the caller's offence from the landlord (Furst & Evans, 2017).

Coping with the Criminal Stigma

Stigma resistance and optimism may reduce the effect of stigma with respect to social withdrawal and isolation following a period of incarceration (Moore, Stuewig & Tangney, 2013, 2016; Moore & Tangney, 2017).

Applying for a pardon or a criminal record suspension offers a hope of removing or significantly mitigating the impacts of a criminal record. However, that avenue is not open to everyone and is only available after a set period of time without a new criminal conviction. In one study, record clearing interventions increased employment rates and average real earnings, often after a period of suppressed earnings (Selbin, McCrary & Epstein, 2018). In a study of 40 persons with a record of past convictions, Adams, Chen and Chapman (2017) found that record clearance benefited ex-offenders through external effects, such as the reduction of barriers to employment, and internal processes, such as the facilitation of cognitive transformation and the affirmation of a new identity.

During our interviews with people presently applying for a criminal record suspension we observed that some of them were in fact ambivalent about applying. For some, it was a matter of avoiding reconnecting psychologically with a criminal past even if they could see the practical benefit of doing so. For others, it was the prospect of having to cope with an unsympathetic bureaucracy or the fear that their application may be rejected.

In another context, interviews with people who had been deemed ineligible for a criminal record expungement expressed distress about the fact that their criminal record could follow them throughout their lives, subjecting them to ongoing stigma (Ispa-Landa, 2019; Ispa-Landa & Loeffler, 2016).

4

Spoiled Identities and Related Hardship

Many of the people we consulted for this study belonged to one or more groups that are frequently stigmatized. In this chapter, we consider the experience of seven of these groups: neurodiverse individuals, people suffering from mental illness or addiction, houseless individuals, crime victims, so-called at-risk youth, women involved in the sex economy, and children with incarcerated parents.

The research findings and testimonies that we present in this chapter may seem repetitive. Indeed, these diverse groups share many similar experiences. Moreover, many people share more than one stigmatized identity. However, the challenges they face and the manner in which they respond to them are not necessarily identical. For example, depending on the extent to which a stigma is concealable, stigmatized individuals have different options in terms of how to respond to it. It may also possibly be easier to avoid or evade stigmatization by resolving a situation of homelessness than by trying to address and heal from a substance use disorder.

Neurodiversity

Neurodiverse individuals are at elevated risk of experiencing stigma, prejudices, and discrimination. Negative attitudes towards people living with autism (Cremin et al., 2021) or attention deficit hyperactivity disorder (Mueller et al., 2012; Visser et al., 2024) are often based on the population's limited knowledge of these conditions, including a problematic or inaccurate understanding of their neurobiological basis and how they manifest differently in individuals. The affective components of these negative attitudes may include anxiety or nervousness about interacting with autistic or other neurodiverse individuals (Engel & Sheppard, 2020).

The resulting stigma leads to discrimination and social isolation, often hindering the individual's ability to access support and treatment. Interestingly, in these situations the stigma is not necessarily related to specific characteristics of the individuals, but rather to behaviour that may be hard for others to understand and accept. Researchers sometimes refer to the double empathy problem, or the idea that when people with very different experiences of the world interact with one another, they will struggle to understand and empathize with each other (Milton, 2012). That explanation emphasizes the communication challenges that exist between neurodiverse and neurotypical people. It suggests that negative attitudes and behaviours are often exacerbated through differences in language use and comprehension.

According to this line of thinking, the stigma experienced by neurodiverse people reflects a breakdown in understanding between themselves and people who experience the world differently. However, as would be expected, various other factors can compound that misunderstanding, including the misperception that either the individuals or their environments are to be blamed for their condition, or the debate about the immediate and long-term effects of the prescribed medication in such instances. An individual who participated in one of our focus group discussions said: "I am tired of having to argue with people around me about what ADHD really is, or the idea that I should be able to control it".

At another level, as self-acceptance is typically a precondition to gaining and feeling social acceptance, including acceptance by significant others, it is hardly surprising that an autism spectrum or ADHD diagnosis can be experienced by many as a liberating moment. The new knowledge that part of one's behaviour may be the result of neurodiversity, a condition which one can begin to explain to oneself or others, makes it possible to reinterpret one's life experience in a more positive light, alleviating feelings of shame, guilt, and responsibility. In the process, individuals may also gain a greater insight into how they have experienced and coped with stigma, the judgment of others, and exclusion. "I finally realized", one neurodiverse person shared with us, "that it is okay to be me."

Nonetheless, neurodiverse people and their family are often ambivalent about seeking a formal diagnosis of that condition. Some of that ambivalence is explainable by the anticipation of stigma. During a focus group discussion with parents of autistic children we encountered young parents, originally from South Asia, who had been not only advised by a pediatrician to refrain from seeking a formal diagnosis for their daughter, but also told not to worry about the condition as it would go away by itself. The doctor suggested to the parents that a formal diagnosis would be more difficult for the girl to conceal and therefore affect her chances of getting a husband.

Mental Illness and Addiction

The mental health stigma is powerful and pervasive, rooted in fear, misunderstanding, and ignorance. People who suffer from a known or presumed mental illness routinely face stigmatization. Stigma poses one of the greatest challenges they face due to its debilitating effects in several life domains.

The stigma varies depending on the type of mental problem, the extent to which it may be concealed and the manners in which it manifests itself and is socially understood (Rüsch, Angermeyer & Corrigan, 2005). Affected individuals are negatively stereotyped, face social rejection, and experience prejudice and discrimination. Conversely, some people are stigmatized because their mental health problem is not acknowledged by others, for example someone whose work performance has been affected by depression and is labelled as lazy or unreliable.

People suffering from a mental health problem are not only harmed by the enacted stigma they experience but also at risk of internalizing it (Chan et al., 2022). Whether stigma is enacted or only anticipated, the resulting self-stigmatizing beliefs can lead to withdrawal from social support, rejection of help, avoidance of treatment, treatment withdrawal, and limited prospects for recovery (Agterberg, 2018).

Sometimes the stigma itself contributes to the person's illness. For example, a study of people who self-identified with mental illness, using the Why Try Stigma Scale (WTSS) and measures of self-stigma and depression, found that the regressive model of self-stigma (aware, agree, apply, harm) worsened individuals' sense of worthiness, which in turn affected personal capability and resulted in increased depression (Corrigan, Nieweglowski & Sayer, 2019).

The decision to seek professional help for a mental health problem is closely related to prevalent public attitudes and beliefs (Angermeyer & Schomerus, 2017). Perceived stigma is related to greater self-stigma and self-stigma affects people's decision to disclose their mental illness to others or to seek help (Corrigan et al., 2010; Corrigan & Rao, 2012). Enacted and internalized stigmas adversely affect recovery attitudes among people with mental illness. Self-stigma is linked to lower recovery orientation followed by lesser service engagement and poorer clinical and functional recovery (Chan et al., 2022). Numerous studies have revealed how the mental health stigma, particularly when internalized, affects people's help-seeking behaviour, adherence to treatment, service engagement, and recovery (Agterberg, 2018; Bowen & Bungay, 2016; Carrara & Ventura, 2018; Farrugia et al., 2021; Lannin et al., 2015; 2017; Stone, 2015).

Stigma is used to control, exclude, and sometimes exploit people with mental illness (Link & Phelan, 2014). For example, the mental health stigma was found to be related to significant employer discrimination against applicants with mental illness (Hipes et al., 2016; Brouwers, 2020). In fact, social stigma is an underestimated contributing factor to unemployment in people with mental illness or other mental health issues. Additionally, anticipated discrimination, self-stigma and the "why try" effect can also lead to unemployment (Brouwers, 2020).

The mental illness stigma across the healthcare spectrum often results in feelings of rejection and being undeserving of care (Conklin, 2021). We will have an opportunity, in Chapter 5, to further examine this particularly harmful consequence of stigma.

Substance Use Disorder

We also know that stigma acts as a barrier to accessing substance use disorder support services, completing treatment, and managing recovery (Burgess et al., 2021; Stone, 2015).

The stronger the public stigma is, the higher is the risk of self-stigma. Yet, substance use disorder triggers one of the harshest and most unforgiving forms of mental health stigmatization in our society. As would be expected, the stigma experienced by those who suffer from that disorder affects their ability to enter treatment and stay in recovery (Burgess et al., 2021). A review of empirical studies on the impacts of perceived stigma and self-stigma on the process of recovering from substance use disorders confirmed that stigmatization experiences are common among those with these disorders. These experiences can negatively impact feelings and beliefs about treatment (Crapanzano et al., 2018). There is also evidence that suggests an indirect effect of stigma on treatment outcomes via negative emotions and cognitive mechanisms such as feelings of self-efficacy (Crapanzano et al., 2018).

What is particularly alarming is the unmistakable evidence that service providers, hospitals and pharmacies are among the primary locations where the addiction stigma is experienced (Burgess et al., 2021). People who inject drugs sometimes feel stigmatized in their interactions with first responders and hospital staff, which they associated with delayed and inadequate medical care for overdoses and injection-related infections (Paquette, Syvertsen & Pollini, 2018). Various meta-studies have concluded that the attitudes of healthcare and other helping professionals continue to contribute to the stigmatizing of people with addiction issues, especially those facing compounded stigma (e.g., Van Boekel, 2013; Rayson & Alba, 2019; Carrara, Bobbili & Ventura, 2023).

Gambling Disorder

A gambling disorder is also a heavily stigmatized mental health problem. People with gambling problems attract substantial negative stereotypes, social distancing, emotional reactions, status loss and discrimination (Dhillon, Horch & Hodgins, 2011; Hing, Russell & Gainsbury, 2016; Dąbrowska & Wieczorek, 2020). They frequently experience anxiety associated with the fear that their condition may be identified and that they may be negatively judged and rejected. They tend to conceal their disorder, which may hinder their treatment (Dąbrowska & Wieczorek, 2020).

Many gamblers internalize the stigma, with deleterious effects on self-esteem, self-efficacy, perceived social worth, and mental and physical health. According to one study, deep shame often exacerbated by relapse was typical among gamblers, and high-risk gamblers were at increased risk of suicidality (Livingstone & Rintoul, 2021).

Problem gambling is often less likely to be considered a mental health disorder than a sign of bad character or moral failure. The situation of the people coping with problem gambling is often concealable. Secrecy therefore appears to be the main coping mechanism used by problem gamblers, with both perceived and self-stigmas acting as major barriers to disclosure and help-seeking (Hing et al., 2015; Hing et al., 2013; Hing & Russel, 2017; Andrà et al., 2022).

Homelessness

It is hardly surprising to learn that the mental health stigma is linked to housing difficulties, well-being outcomes, and homelessness (Mejia-Lancheros et al., 2021). However, there is also stigma attached to homelessness itself, a stigma that intersects with other stigmas, such as mental illness, race, or addiction. People experiencing homelessness endure personal and economic hardships as well as discrimination and exclusion. Experiencing homelessness is associated with poor health, high levels of chronic disease and premature mortality.

While research has long demonstrated the medical and psychological consequences of being chronically or temporarily homeless, less attention has been paid to the debilitating stigma surrounding homelessness and the resulting barriers in accessing services (Begum et al., 2024; Omeroy et al., 2020). That stigma is reflected in the way society, lawmakers, police, and the healthcare system interact with people experiencing homelessness. It creates additional barriers to stable housing and employment and worsens mental health issues.

To avoid being stigmatized, some people who are experiencing homelessness try to keep their housing status secret. Like other people occupying concealable stigmatized identities, they often prefer not to disclose their stigmatized status, and this usually exacerbates feelings of isolation and reduced perceptions of social support (Rea, 2023). As a result, they are unable to enroll in services or find housing within their social network. They may also avoid entering public spaces for fear of being ridiculed or harassed. As such, they become further marginalized, and their struggle to meet their basic needs of food, clothing and shelter becomes overwhelming.

People experiencing homelessness tend to face highly legitimized forms of discrimination, amplifying negative wellbeing consequences. Because one's housing status is perceived as somewhat under one's control, people experiencing homelessness are often perceived as solely responsible for their lack of adequate housing (Johnstone et al., 2015).

Based on a systematic review of the research on the homeless stigma and its impacts, Johanna Reilly and her colleagues found clear evidence that perceived stigma related to homelessness correlates with poorer mental and physical health (Reilley et al., 2022). They also found persistent evidence that experiencing homelessness is linked to stigmatization by health care providers and impacts general access to care and support services (Reilley et al., 2022). The stigma and discrimination experienced in healthcare settings were identified as a barrier to care. For example, women with children who were staying in shelters have reported being monitored by shelter and agency staff and feeling stigmatized as "bad mothers" or unknowledgeable about what is best for their children because they are without a home (Canham et al., 2024).

People experiencing homelessness use various strategies to cope with the homeless stigma and construct a positive self-identity. For example, some of them actively construct a self-identity and convey a public image as entrepreneurs through routine recycling work that they present as socially valuable (Johnstone et al., 2015). They are possibly also less likely to identify with other homeless people. They may have limited opportunities to join groups that can protect their wellbeing when facing discrimination. Homeless people who need such identity resources may not always access them because stigma and discrimination act as barriers against building social connections.

Social connections and the associated social support are instrumental in protecting individuals against the stressful experience of homelessness. However, people experiencing homelessness speak of relationship difficulties and social isolation both prior to and throughout their experience of homelessness. Relationship breakdown may result in less social support and the person's reluctance to access much needed relational support, including from family, friends and support workers (Rea, 2023). At the same time, as people attempt to keep their homelessness a secret, their sense of isolation is exacerbated, leading to feelings of depression, anxiety and a loss of confidence.

Victimization

In recent years, victim support interventions have been strengthened by adopting a trauma-informed approach, but they have yet to fully integrate the knowledge on the impact of various stigmas that often accompany the experience of victimization. Stigma is known as a major determinant of behaviour, health and well-being among vulnerable and marginalized victims of violence and their families. It is known to have a debilitating effect on individuals who experience stigmatization because of sexual exploitation, intimate partner violence (IPV), and other forms of victimization. These effects lead these victims to develop concealment, self-protection, self-isolation, and risk management tendencies that are not particularly healthy and can hinder recovery. There is therefore a need for a stigma-informed approach to victim assistance.

The stigma attached to victimization is sometimes only one aspect of the victims' stigmatized identities (intersecting stigmas). Its impact is often compounded by the effects of other stigmas associated with obesity, substance abuse, cultural stereotypes, racism, mental health, pregnancy, even the stigma attached to place (e.g., coming from the wrong side of the track).

The anticipation of stigma and shame is a major reason why so many victimization incidents are never reported to the police. For example, one may note that the shame of having been deceived by some con-artist and being perceived as gullible is enough to dissuade many victims of fraud and financial crimes from reporting to the authorities. Anticipated stigmatization is a critical reason why individuals conceal their personal situation or victimization from others and hesitate to seek help. It leads the victims to avoid or withdraw from situations in which there is the potential for discrimination. That, in turn, negatively impacts behaviour, social relationships, and functioning (Murray, Crowe & Overstreet, 2018; Murray, Crowe & Brinkley, 2015; Overstreet & Quinn, 2013).

Victim stigmatization takes many forms. These include shame, blame, and denying their victimhood status because they do not fit the "ideal victim" stereotype. For example, a person's claim to victimhood may be denied because she works in the sex economy, has a criminal record, or is struggling with addiction. Also, people often entertain unrealistic expectations about victims and how they could have avoided victimization. Many people assume that the victim's situation is volitional and therefore escapable.

The effects of stigma often continue long after the victimization has stopped. For instance, research has begun to reveal the plight of victims of intimate partner violence IPV through a more complex stigma framework (Eckstein, 2015; Murray, Crowe & Overstreet, 2015; Overstreet & Quinn, 2013; Overstreet et al., 2017). The stigmatization of IPV victims, based on beliefs that victims are passive, emotionally dependent, flawed, weak, or deserving of their own victimization, often results in status loss, victim-blame, and victim stereotyping. This influences how victims attribute meaning to their victimization experience in relation to the self (self-identity) (Overstreet & Quinn, 2013). The stigma is often internalized by IPV victims, leading to feelings of blame, shame, guilt, and inferiority directed towards the self (Murray, Crowe & Overstreet, 2015). The internalization of stigma seems to be influenced by the centrality of the victimization experience, that is the importance and personal meaning of the victimization to one's identity or self-concept (Overstreet et al., 2017). We thus begin to understand why, for some victims, the stigma associated with their victimization is something that is "tagged on" to their identity. Their identity has been spoiled by the reaction of others.

That spoiled identity is both debilitating and a barrier to help seeking (Overstreet & Quinn, 2013). When victims lose their certainty about who they are, whom they love or must love, what they must honour and what they need to do to be accepted and to belong, they become vulnerable and disempowered. We know the struggle that many victims go through as they refuse to be defined by their victimization. One woman talked to us about her struggle to regain a measure of self-confidence and agency after her victimization. She confided: "I don't want to be a victim. I know I have to let go of that." For many victims, identifying oneself as a "survivor" rather than as a victim is part of an effort to avoid stigmatization and the negative feelings that come with it.

You may have observed already that, in abusive relationships, abusers can use both social stigma and self-stigma to control the victims by manipulating their fear of social judgment, rejection and exclusion. For example, in cases involving intimate partner violence or sexual offences, the abusers may use the victims' fear of the judgment of others and the anticipated stigma to control them and provoke situations to damage their reputation in the eyes of their friends, relatives, and even children. You may think here of situations where the abusers use social media to vilify the victims, expose them to various forms of indignity, isolate them from those who could offer them support, or implicitly justify the violence they perpetrated.

We can see therefore how stigma is a tool of both social and individual control (Tyler & Slater, 2018). Some research refers to *stigma power* when someone is trying to control another person by using stigma or anticipated stigma. Stigma power refers to instances in which stigma processes achieve the aims of stigmatizers with respect to the exploitation, control or exclusion of others (Link & Phelan, 2014). The concept of stigma power shifts the conventional understanding of stigma as an individual psychological process toward a more complex conceptualization of it as "a set of internal and external social processes, affecting multiple domains of people's lives" (Benoit, Jansson, Smith & Flagg, 2018).

SSelf-stigma and anticipated stigma among crime victims lead to withdrawal, social distancing, isolation and disengaged living, and therefore affect the victims' quality of life (Yip et al., 2023). Moreover, many victims related to us how, following their victimization, they faced various forms of subtle exclusion and micro-aggression in their immediate social environment. They also said that they did not know how to respond to them.

At-risk Youth

The construction and labelling of some young people as "risky" or "troubled" are driven by frequent reporting in the popular press about so-called out-of-control or anti-social young people. These discourses produce and reproduce negative labels and stereotypes that drive disadvantage and trigger a multifaceted stigmatization process (Deakin et al., 2020). The "at-risk" label has made disadvantaged youth the target of increasingly punitive and controlling policies and practices, and "resulted in a variety of responses from young people including various forms of resistance" (Harragan et al., 2018: 2)

Simply being identified as part of a group of youth at risk can be the beginning of a long stigmatization and discrimination process. Keep in mind that many youth crime prevention initiatives are typically planned around so-called risk factors based on statistical associations at the group level between those factors and problem behaviour. That approach is used to identify not only the risk factors but also the individuals to be targeted by various interventions. In effect, it serves to justify interventions that single out and target various vulnerable or marginalized youth groups. This typically leads to a very expansive definition of risk factors and, ultimately, the targeting and potential stigmatization of "problem children" and their families (Case, 2007; Case & Haines, 2010).

Prevention interventions based on that approach align with a deficit model of youth which posits that young people from disadvantaged groups are uniformly deficient and in need of development. Crime is reduced to a putative individual social adaptation issue, and at-risk youth are deemed to be more inclined towards antisocial or criminal behaviour, whether because of their milieu, their uncaring or incompetent parents, or some other developmental deficit (Dandurand & Heidt, 2023).

That risk management approach to youth crime prevention, based on uncritical assumptions and flawed measurement of the risk they represent, further stigmatizes youth from various marginalized groups (Dandurand & Heidt, 2023). Since the focus is on individual risk factors such as low intelligence, low empathy, impulsiveness, family problems, abuse, and neglect, "the proposed methods of interventions typically consist of targeted and intensive work with 'problem children' and their families" (Garside, 2009: 42). Interventions such as increased surveillance, reduced opportunities, negative interactions, curfews, or incarceration simply exacerbates the cycle of stigma (Deakin, Fox & Matos, 2022). These youth saving interventions, irrespective of their intent, are very detrimental to the youth they purposefully or inadvertently stigmatize.

Fighting off and coping with stigmas based on statistical speculation is a huge challenge for many disadvantaged or marginalized youth. Their experience of navigating fraught relationships with authorities and facing interventions designed to manage their behaviour deserves to be better understood.

Sex Work

The stigma attached to sex work is a major challenge for people engaged in it, including those hoping to exit the sex economy (Benoit et al., 2018, 2018a, 2020). Moreover, stigmatized identities do not exist in a vacuum: intersecting forms of stigma (intersectional stigma) are a daily reality for sex workers and expose them to a broad range of vulnerabilities and risks (Turan et al., 2019). Many sex workers face the triple social disapproval and stigmas associated with prostitution, addiction and criminal behaviour. These stigmas are at play at three levels: structural stigma, public stigma, and self-stigma (Blakey & Gunn, 2018).

A Vancouver study involving semi-structured interviews with 26 cisgender and five transgender women street-based sex workers about their working conditions indicated that despite police rhetoric of prioritizing sex workers' safety, these individuals were denied police protection by virtue of their risky occupation and were thus responsibilized for the violence they experienced (Krüsi et al., 2016). Sex workers' interactions with neighbourhood residents were predominantly shaped by a discourse of sex workers as a "risky presence" in the urban landscape and police took swift action in removing sex workers in the case of complaints (Krüsi et al., 2016).

Stigma and the associated discrimination and exclusion have an impact on the sex worker's individual's identity, self-concept, self-confidence, agency and overall ability to seek and receive assistance (Benoit et al., 2018a). The stigma surrounding sex also has a significant impact on the sex workers' mental health (Benoit, McCarthy & Jansson, 2015, 2015a; Carlson, 2017; Weitzer, 2018; Rayson & Alba, 2019; Treolar et al., 2021; Turan et al., 2019).

Some studies have shown that perceived stigma is pronounced among those who work in the sex industry and negatively affects health independently of sex work involvement (e.g., Benoit, McCarthy & Jansson, 2015; 2015a). One of these studies showed positive associations between depression and sex work and between discrimination and depression (Benoit, McCarthy & Jansson, 2015). Adult sex workers report notably worse perceived mental health, poorer social determinants of health (except for income) and nearly triple the prevalence of unmet healthcare needs as compared to the general population (Benoit, Ouellet & Jansson, 2016).

Sex workers are faced with the dilemma of disclosure. They often feel compelled to conceal their identities and use various strategies to do so, including withdrawing themselves from social networks (Wong, 2011; Koken, 2012). In some cases, workers attempt complete concealment of their occupation (Ham & Gilmour, 2017). However, this type of closeting poses its own challenges because sex workers must create cover stories to hide their work activities from partners, family, friends, and their community (Benoit, Ouellet & Jansson, 2016). Many of them employ strategies to separate their personal and professional identities and protect their self-image from the stigma of sex work. They often live double lives and try to manage the stigma and the ongoing difficulty of restricting who knows about their work or what they know about it (Benoit, 2019; Armstrong & Fraser, 2020). However, concealing one's activities, maintaining multiple identities and the accompanying need for vigilance and isolation can compound the negative outcomes of stigma (Benoit et al., 2018; Quinn & Earnshaw, 2013; Weitzer, 2018).

Cecilia Benoit and her colleagues (2020), based on interviews conducted with a diverse sample of 218 adult sex workers in Canada, described how these individuals often strategically responded to stigma contingent on the situated contexts of their work and personal life. The researchers identified four main coping approaches among the sex workers they interviewed: (1) some participants internalized negative discourses about their sex work and accepted their discredited status; (2) many of them controlled access to information about themselves, consciously keeping knowledge of their occupation from most people while sharing it with trusted others; (3) some of them rejected society's negative view of their occupation; (4) some attempted to reduce the personal impact of stigma by reframing sex work to emphasise its positive and empowering elements (Benoit et al., 2020).

Stigma has a negative impact on healthcare utilization by sex workers, including utilization of services for HIV prevention and treatment (Oga et al., 2020). Stigma hinders sex workers' health-seeking behaviours. A Canadian study showed that sex workers had mixed feelings about revealing their work status in healthcare encounters. Those who decided not to disclose were fearful of negative treatment or expressed confidentiality concerns or lack of relevancy. Those who divulged their occupational status to a health provider mainly described benefits, including nonjudgment, relationship building, and comprehensive care, while a minority experienced costs that included judgment, stigma, and inappropriate health care (Benoit et al., 2019).

The fear of judgment from healthcare providers is a major factor responsible for sex workers' unmet healthcare needs. Those who have disclosed their occupation to healthcare providers encounter various forms of discrimination, including having insensitive and abusive language used toward them, being treated disrespectfully or humiliated in public healthcare spaces, experiencing physical marginalization within the healthcare setting, denial of care, and breaches of confidentiality

(Benoit, Ouellet & Jansson, 2016). Some sex workers also report poor treatment from mental health practitioners who see them as victims lacking agency, impose beliefs that sex work was the pathological root cause of mental health issues, or approach the issue with fascination or voyeurism (Carlson et al., 2018).

Interviews with eight sex work experts who had experience as sex workers, advocates and service providers revealed how they confronted direct enacted stigma and had become proficient at managing discrediting information about themselves when in the presence of those they mistrusted (Bowen & Bungay, 2016). They supported sex workers through stigmatizing experiences by using knowledge gained from these intersecting direct and vicarious experiences of stigma, while building capacity within themselves and among other sex workers to resist stigma (Bowen & Bungay, 2016).

Associative and Intergenerational Stigma

As we saw earlier, some people experience stigmatization because of their link or association with a stigmatized person (Östman & Kjellin, 2002; Pryor, Reeder & Monroe, 2012). Associative stigma results from a process through which relatives or associates of stigmatized persons are discredited and stigmatized. The channels for associative stigma range from the enduring bonds of kinship to the arbitrary occasions of being seen in the company of a stigmatized individual, including being a member of the same age or ethnic group as the stigmatized individual (Pryor, Reeder & Monroe, 2012).

Social disapproval and stigma are indeed contagious and transferrable. For example, studies have shown that the stigmatization process impacts the social interactions between those who are stigmatized in sex work jobs and other people they are in contact with (e.g., Benoit, Jansson, Smith & Flagg, 2018). Similarly, a peer's recent arrest may increase the risk of an adolescent's arrest because they associate with someone who has been involved in the justice system. Erin Tinney

(2022) wrote about the "stickiness of stigma" and "guilt by association", suggesting that stigma not only sticks from one individual to another but may also persist despite efforts to end one's association with the arrested individual (Tinney, 2022).

People suffering from mental illness are not the sole recipients of stigmatization; their immediate family members may be subjected to stigma by association (Yim et al., 2020). Friends and family members of people suffering from mental illness often experience stigma and its detrimental effects on their wellbeing. Studies have shown that familial relationships, co-residence, and gender may all be factors in the associative stigma experience (van der Sanden et al., 2015). In a Swedish study, most of the relatives of patients in acute psychiatric care revealed that they had experienced the psychological effects of stigma by association (Östman & Kjellin, 2002). These psychological effects were like those experienced by people who had a diagnosis, including a tendency to isolate and avoid social interactions. Some of them withdrew from social situations to avoid having to answer difficult questions about the people they were related to.

You may not even be surprised to learn that, in China, the Qianke (social credit system) instituted by the state, even if it is largely inaccessible to the public, imposes restraints not only on the individuals with a criminal record but also on their families in accessing education, employment and public services. That kind of discrimination is justified by the authorities as driven by a concern with risk prevention (Li, 2023).

It is not farfetched to talk about intergenerational stigma to refer to children who are stigmatized because of their parents' conduct or condition. For instance, there is ample empirical evidence showing that parental incarceration is a serious adverse childhood experience that has a detrimental and frequently traumatic impact on children and their development. Some families find that situation so shameful that they do not tell the children where their parents are or disclose the situation to them. This can lead to feelings of fear, confusion, abandonment and low self-worth. The stigma has a lasting effect on all family relationships (Mitchell, 2024).

Children with incarcerated parents typically report experiences such as consistently moving residences, homelessness, attending multiple schools or an inability to attend school, placement in state care, and a lack of household resources (Shaw, 2013). At the same time, parental incarceration is typically a source of harsh associative stigmatization. Children often experience a transference of stigma as a parent's criminal record becomes a representation of a child's moral worth (Shaw, 2023). Assumptions are made about the child, based on the parent's actions and interactions with the justice system. Once knowledge of parental incarceration spread in a community, stigma can appear in many forms and is highly damaging to the child. Negative attitudes are sometimes displayed by teachers, social workers, community members, and social service or criminal justice practitioners. These can include comments such as "the apple doesn't fall far from the tree," or suggestions that the child will be a negative influence on their peer group (EFry, 2019; Shaw, 2023). Youth crime prevention programs often target these children and youth, as they are assumed to be "at risk".

To make a point about the pervasiveness of the stigma affecting children with an incarcerated parent, as part of a community mobilization project to enhance the protective environment around these children, we often presented meeting participants with the following hypothetical situation. Your 10-year-old daughter is asking for your permission to go to a sleepover at the home of one of her school friends. You know a little about the friend, but you don't know much about her family. After inquiring from a neighbour, you find out that one of the friend's parents is apparently serving time in prison. Do you give your daughter permission to go? In many of these meetings, we could not even find any participant who would answer "yes" to that question.

That kind of stigma by association prevents children from seeking help, connecting with peers, participating in recreational activities, and reaching out to social supports. Children with an incarcerated parent anticipate stigma and often feel shame. We can easily understand why so many of them go to great lengths to conceal that fact from a least some people in their lives (Scharff-Smith, 2014; Griffin et al., 2025). Some of them even change their name.

The effects may be more acute for teenagers. Adolescents, already craving independence, may be more likely to react with anger and a desire to cut off all contacts with the parent (McCormick, Millar & Paddock, 2014). Their reaction may involve engaging in criminal behaviour, inappropriate sexual activity, self-harm, aggression towards others, or substance use (Kjellstrand & Eddy, 2011; Davis & Shlafer, 2017).

5

Gender and Stigma

Gender plays a determining role in how stigmas are generated and applied within different contexts, the impacts they have on individuals, as well as the way in which individuals respond to being stigmatized. Moreover, gender-based stigmas reinforce discrimination, exclusion and inequality, shaping people's experiences based on their gender and intersecting identities.

A gender analysis can help us understand how various stigmas operate differently for men, women, and gender-diverse individuals and expose how gender-related social norms and expectations contribute to the stigmatization and marginalization of individuals and groups. For example, we can observe that, while men may face stigma for expressing vulnerability, women often encounter judgment for defying traditional gender roles. Non-binary and transgender individuals experience compounded discrimination for challenging binary norms. As will be discussed in this chapter, these gendered stigmas affect the welfare and wellbeing of individuals and their own help seeking behaviour, and they hinder their access to healthcare and other support services as well as employment opportunities.

We must remember that stigma serves multiple functions, including reinforcing the dominance of powerful groups by maintaining social inequities and securing their privileged position (Bos et al., 2013:4). Additionally, stigma acts as a tool of social control, using the threat of exclusion to pressure individuals into conforming to accepted societal norms as they seek to be recognized as part of an "in-group" (Bos et al.,

2013: 4). As one examines stigmas through a gendered lens, one can better understand how gender-based power dynamics shape experiences of discrimination and impede access to supports and services.

We begin this chapter by examining gendered stigmas, or the negative social perceptions or prejudice directed towards someone based on their gender. We consider the societal disapproval and negative labeling associated with not conforming to expected gender roles or characteristics. We then consider how men and women are affected and respond differently to social stigmas, how their stigma coping strategies tend to differ, and how that tends to affect their help-seeking behaviour. We conclude the chapter by a few observations about how stigma specifically affects women's desistance from crime and social reintegration.

Gendered Stigmas

Some stigmas have their sources in restrictive gender stereotypes and norms, incorporating the attitudes, behavioural intentions and enacted behaviours that are produced and reinforced by structures and systems that support inequalities (Stewart et al., 2021). Gender-based stereotypes are informed by social norms relating to ideals and practices of masculinity and femininity. They inform our assumptions about others based on their gender.

Gendered stigmas are stereotypes, biases, or negative perceptions assigned to individuals based on their gender. These stigmas may vary across cultures and contexts, and over time, but are rooted in societal biases that unfairly stereotype individuals based on their gender. (Hernandes-Fernandes et al., 2022). For instance, women often face stigmas related to leadership and assertiveness, being labeled as "bossy" or "too aggressive" when exhibiting traits that are praised in men, such as confidence. Men, on the other hand, may encounter stigmas when expressing vulnerability or engaging in traditionally feminine roles, such as caregiving or emotional openness, which are wrongly viewed as signs of weakness. Non-binary and transgender individuals face additional stigmas, as they challenge conventional gender norms, often being subjected to misunderstanding, exclusion, or discrimination. These stigmas perpetuate inequality, restrict individual expression, and reinforce harmful stereotypes that impact both personal and professional lives.

The following are some examples of gendered stigmas that women commonly face:

Emotionality and Mental Health: Women are often stereotyped as overly emotional or irrational.

Motherhood and Career Ambition: Women who prioritize their careers over motherhood may be judged as selfish or neglectful, while stay at home mothers may face stigma for not being ambitious.

Sexuality and Purity: Women are frequently subjected to a double standard regarding sexuality. Women who are sexually active may be labeled as promiscuous, while those who are not may be viewed as unattractive or undesirable.

Aging and Appearance: Women are often valued primarily for their youth and beauty, leading to stigma against aging women, who may be seen as being less worthy of attention.

Survivors of Sexual Violence: Women who experience sexual assault or harassment often face victim blaming, where they are questioned about their clothing, behaviour, or choices, rather than focusing on the offender's actions.

Women and Substance Use: Women who struggle with problematic substance use often face harsher judgement than men, as substance use is seen as conflicting with their traditional female caregiving role and their family responsibility.

Contrast the above with the following examples of gendered stigmas encountered by men:

Emotional Expression: Men are often expected to be stoic and emotionally strong. Crying and expressing vulnerability may be stigmatized as a form of weakness or a failure to meet traditional masculine standards.

Mental Health and Help-Seeking: Seeking therapy or admitting to struggles with anxiety, depression, or trauma is often seen as unmanly and a sign of weakness.

Caregiving and Fatherhood: Men who take on caregiving roles, such as stay-at-home fathers, may face stigma for not conforming to the traditional breadwinner role, with some viewing them as less competent or unmanly.

Survivors of Abuse or Assault: Men who experience domestic violence, sexual assault, or other forms of abuse often face stigma and disbelief, as societal narratives tend to depict men as aggressors rather than victims and view male victims as lacking in masculinity and displaying weakness.

Professional and Financial Expectations: Men are often expected to be providers, and those who struggle financially face stigma for not fulfilling the traditional role.

Aggression and Strength: While men are often expected to be strong and assertive, they may also face stigma if they are perceived as too aggressive, violent, or emotionally detached, leading to a narrow and contradictory definition of acceptable masculinity. On the other hand, men who are perceived as being not aggressive enough may be labeled as weak or lacking in manly qualities.

Women often face stigmas that undermine their competence, such as with motherhood and the societal expectations related to being committed to caring and nurturing their family and children. In contrast, men are often stigmatized for stepping outside traditional masculinity, such as showing vulnerability, seeking mental health support, or pursuing careers in caregiving fields, like nursing or teaching.

Additionally, there are gender differences in how these stigmas are perceived, as women may feel heightened pressure to conform to appearance-based standards, while men might experience shame or silence when confronting stigmas tied to emotional expression. These differences not only shape behaviour but also reinforce systemic inequities, making it harder for both genders to break free from societal expectations. While both genders face stigmas, the nature and impact of these stigmas are shaped by cultural gender norms and societal expectations. Addressing these disparities requires a nuanced approach that considers the intersectionality of gender, social roles, and other identities. Gender-based stigma can intersect with other identities (race, class, sexual orientation), amplifying its effects. For example, BIPOC women may face compounded stigmas tied to both gender and racial stereotypes.

Finally, here are some examples of gendered stigmas that affect non-binary and transgender individuals:

Legitimacy of Identity: Non-binary and transgender individuals often face stigma rooted in the belief that their identities are "not real," "a phase," or "confusing," leading to frequent invalidation and misgendering.

Social and Workplace Discrimination: Many non-binary and transgender individuals face stigma in professional and public spaces, where they may be excluded, denied opportunities, or pressured to conform to gender norms through dress codes or pronoun use.

Medical and Healthcare Barriers: Trans individuals often experience stigma in healthcare settings, including providers refusing to acknowledge their gender identity, and lack of access to gender-affirming care.

Violence and Safety Concerns: Non-binary and transgender individuals, particularly transgender BIPOC women, face disproportionately high rates of violence, hate crimes, and harassment, fueled by social stigma and transphobia.

Perceptions of Deception – Trans individuals, especially trans women, may face the harmful stereotype that they are being deceptive about their gender, leading to dangerous social and legal consequences, including increased vulnerability to violence.

Body and Appearance Stigma: Non-binary and trans individuals often experience stigma related to their physical appearance, facing pressure to look like a man or a woman, and criticism if they do not conform to what society views as normal.

Legal and Institutional Barriers: Stigma manifests in legal norms and systems that refuse to recognize non-binary genders, making it difficult for individuals to obtain accurate identification documents or legal protections.

How Stigma Affects Women and Men Differently

Stigmas affect men and women differently due to social expectations, cultural norms, and power dynamics. Men and women are affected differently by stigmas due to societal expectations tied to traditional gender roles. Society expects women to be nurturing, caring, and to take care of the home and children, and avoid partaking in activities that are socially deemed unacceptable for women, such as promiscuity, as they are deemed unladylike, and to which great shame is attached.

A study by Davern and colleagues showed how perceived stigma among acne sufferers can significantly contribute to health-related quality of life, psychological distress, and somatic symptoms (Davern, O'Donnell & Picardo, 2018). Gender was found to be significantly correlated with both health-related quality of life and somatic symptoms. Women were found to experience greater life quality impairment and more symptoms than males, possibly because females encounter increased social pressure to possess clear skin and are possibly more concerned about the appearance than males (Davern, O'Donnell & Picardo, 2018).

Having a gambling problem may be seen as incompatible with women's historically defined gender roles (e.g. caregivers and nurturers) and attracts judgments such as being irresponsible (Hing & Russel, 2017). Similarly, men and women are affected differently by weight-stigma experiences, and weight stigma is related to lower levels of motivation to exercise in overweight and obese individuals (Sattler et al., 2018). Research also showed that men and women are affected differently by the stigma associated with physical disability:

> "For instance, whereas men's disability stereotypically connotes loss of masculinity, agency, and responsibility, women's disability stereotypically raises issues of dependency, passivity, and loss of attractiveness and desirability" (Mimoun & Margalit, 2023: 80).

One study found that women were blamed and stigmatized more than men when diagnosed with HIV/AIDS, as it was assumed that they had deviated from what would be considered socially acceptable behaviour for a woman, and thus contracted the virus, while with men, the diagnosis was more accepted, as it was suggested that "misbehaviour is to be expected and tolerated" (Asiedu et al., 2014). In another study, men and women both reported modifying their behaviour due to anticipated stigma and disclosed internalized stigma, describing shame, guilt and depression over their HIV status (Celeste-Villalvir et al., 2023). However, only women discussed isolating themselves and experiencing discomfort taking HIV medication in front of others. These experiences were more common among women and women who had been diagnosed with HIV/AIDS faced more rejection from family and friends, as well as an increased incidence of physical abuse, violence, and sexual assault after their diagnosis (Celeste-Villalvir et al., 2023).

Similarly, various studies have documented significant gender differences in the experience of stigma among people struggling with a substance use disorder (Burgess et al., 2021; Celeste-Villalvir et al., 2023). External and internalized stigma are among the female-specific barriers to accessing alcohol use disorder treatment, together with lack of childcare and systemic barriers. This may partly explain, as some researchers have suggested, why women tend to be more isolated in their excessive alcohol use and recovery and are more likely than men to believe their alcohol problem will resolve on its own (Glanton, Cucciate & Epstein, 2020).

Given the gendered expectations regarding parenting, individuals often face moral judgements and stigmas with respect to their parental behaviour – e.g., the "bad mother", the "dead beat dad." Social expectations regarding responsible parenting are not only culturally defined, but also heavily class-based (Hays, 1996). For women, motherhood begins with pregnancy and various stigmas are attached to their behaviour and attitude during that period. Teenage mothers, for instance, are aware of the stigmas and cultural stereotypes surrounding young, working-class mothers.

Some studies have found that mothers of children with fetal alcohol spectrum disorder (FASD) are highly stigmatized for their past behaviour (Corrigan et al., 2017). There is also the stigma directed at pregnant women dependent on opioids. That stigma was one of the main barriers to seeking and receiving substance abuse treatment reported among pregnant women in rural communities (Jackson & Shannon, 2012). A pregnant woman who has a substance use disorder is doubly stigmatized: as an "addict" and as a "bad mother" (Howard, 2015). These women report experiencing anxiety, guilt, worry and concern. They tend to try to maintain secrecy around their situation, especially in a case of relapse (Howard, 2015). Many of them fear that their previous drug use (or imprisonment) may become known to their children (Sharpe, 2024).

Many women fear or face judgements of maternal deficiency for failing to meet cultural expectations regarding respectable or responsible child rearing – the "bad mother" stigma (Morris, 2018). Some of them are silenced through the stigma and shame of being judged as flawed mothers and the fear of child protection services' interventions and court-ordered restrictions. Removal of one's children is devastating. Women who have lost custody of their children following a court order often struggle to free themselves from the bad mother stigma and the shame of being considered an unfit mother, in the hope of a future reunification with their children (Morris, 2018). Perceptions of negative appraisal and stigma often hinders these mothers' access to services for themselves as well as for their children (Sharpe, 2024). There is also the welfare stigma attached to mothers who claim social security benefits, the perception that benefits are undeserved and the notion that recipients are incompetent mothers (Evans, 2022).

Young mothers with a history of lawbreaking, as well as other markers of a spoiled past, typically encounter various forms of gendered surveillance, social censure and stigma across multiple domains of identity. Many of them, regardless of whether they are currently involved in crime, continue to be stigmatized as maternally deficient long after they have desisted from crime (Sharpe, 2015). Judgements of maternal deficiency frequently cast a "long shadow" that lasts for years (Sharpe, 2024: 78).

A study on the response to the stigma attached to depression among medical students in China found that male participants were twice as likely as female participants to state that they would not "make friends" with or even "try to avoid" someone suffering from depression (Qiu et al., 2022: 4). This suggests that men may view mental health issues in a more negative light than women do, at least in Chinese culture. Krystal Sattler and her colleagues (2018) examined gender differences in weight-based stigmatization and its impacts on motivation to exercise or engage in physical activity. They found that women experienced more negative impacts on mental and physical health, as they generally faced more weight related stigma than men. Findings such as those highlight the fact that men and women experience social stigmas differently and are affected by and often respond differently to that experience.

There is less research on the impacts of gendered stigma on non-binary and transgender individuals. However, one may note that non-binary and transgender individuals face compounded gendered stigmas related to mental health, substance use, and trauma, often rooted in societal rejection of their gender identities. They are frequently stigmatized as being "confused", "unnatural" or "attention-seeking", which invalidates their experiences and creates significant barriers to accessing mental health care. This stigma can exacerbate feelings of isolation and discrimination, contributing to higher rates of anxiety, depression, and suicidal ideation.

Additionally, transgender, and non-binary individuals are disproportionately affected by trauma, including physical violence, sexual assault, and systemic discrimination, yet stigma surrounding their identities often leads to their victimization being dismissed or minimized. These intersecting stigmas create unique challenges that require affirming, trauma-informed, and inclusive care to address the mental health and substance use needs of transgender and non-binary individuals. For non-binary and gender-nonconforming individuals, there is the assumption that everyone fits into the categories of male or female, leading to stigma or exclusion for those who do not. We often see gender diverse individuals experiencing stigma or backlash for using pronouns or expressing identities that are outside of the traditional gender norms

Gender and Stigma Coping Strategies, Including Disclosure

Gender significantly influences how individuals cope or fail to cope with stigmas, as societal expectations shape the strategies acceptable for men and women. Women, for example, often rely on social networks for support, using advocacy or shared experiences to challenge stigmas, particularly those related to gender inequality or appearance. More than men, women face caregiver obligations and challenges. Connections to family and friends who provide instrumental and emotional support are especially important to women (Stone et al., 2018). Men, on the other hand, may struggle to cope with stigmas tied to vulnerability or failure, as traditional masculinity discourages seeking help or freely addressing emotional struggles. This often leads to internalized stress or avoidance strategies, such as overcompensation through assertiveness or silence.

Mimoun and Margalit (2023) studied the disclosure of an invisible disability to a romantic partner and the differences experienced between men and women. Men faced stigma related to a loss of their masculinity, agency, and responsibility, while women faced stigma related to issues of dependency, agency, and loss of attractiveness (Mimoun & Margalit, 2023: 64). The decision to self-disclose requires weighing these risks against potential benefits, such as receiving support, breaking down stigma, and fostering more open conversations about mental health and social issues. Addressing these gendered barriers requires creating safe, judgment-free spaces where both men and women feel empowered to share their experiences without fear of stigma or discrimination.

Because HIV stigma and people's coping strategies are influenced by the sociocultural context, several studies have examined the perceived stigma associated with HIV and the coping strategies used in the context of gender. Men and women living with HIV have different experiences with both HIV-related perceived stigma and coping strategies used. Women reported a higher level of disclosure stigma than men and the types of coping strategies used vary between male and female (Ataro et al., 2020).

A cross-sectional study that compared gender differences in how people coped with HIV/AIDS related stigmas found that women were more likely to use emotional support and religion, while men were more likely to turn to humour (Ataro et al., 2020). The study also revealed that women tended to experience a higher level of stigma then men after disclosing their condition and thus were more likely to refrain from disclosing their status for fear of the resulting bias (Ataro et al., 2020). It appeared that women chose non-disclosure of their condition as a means of avoiding stigmatization, even if it affected their health. The same study also revealed that men were more likely than women to resort to substance use to cope with the HIV/AIDS related stigma, while women tended to disengage from social relationships and seek self-distraction through various means.

A more recent study (Celeste-Villalvir et al., 2023) reported that men and women both engaged in adjusting their behaviour because of anticipated HIV/AIDS related stigma, but women were more likely to engage in self isolation and suicidal ideation, while men focused on blaming others for their diagnosis and expressed a desire to move on.

Making the choice to self-disclose personal experiences, such as HIV/AIDS status, mental health struggles, trauma, or substance use, is often complicated by stigma. Men may hesitate to disclose vulnerabilities due to societal expectations of toughness and self-reliance, fearing they will be perceived as weak or incapable (Gerrish, 2021). This can lead to isolation and reluctance to seek help, worsening mental health conditions or delaying recovery. Women, on the other hand, may face stigma that frames their struggles as signs of instability or incompetence, particularly in professional settings, where they risk being dismissed or treated differently. Survivors of trauma, especially women who have experienced sexual violence, often fear being blamed, shamed, or discredited if they come forward. In Ghana, a study of gender differences in HIV/AIDS related stigma experiences revealed gender differences in how individuals disclosed their serostatus, an indicator of HIV infection (Asiedu & Myers-Bowman, 2014). It appeared that women were stigmatized more than men because women often voluntarily disclosed their status, whereas men did not. Women apparently disclose their status to receive support (financial or emotional), whereas men were too proud to disclose or did not see the need. People also reacted to women's diagnoses differently than to men's (Asiedu & Myers-Bowman, 2014).

Internalized stigma, shame and guilt lead explains why women under-report any substance misuse during their pregnancy, thus affecting their access to specialized prenatal care (Paris et al., 2020). Paris and colleagues identified four themes related to women's decision to disclose problematic substance use during pregnancy: (1) secrecy for fear of shame, guilt and judgement, (2) using avoidance, manipulation, and lying to keep their substance use secret, (3) choosing disclosure out of concern for the unborn baby, recognizing a need for help, and identifying that change was needed, and (4) how and who they chose to disclose to, such as advising healthcare professionals and/or family (Paris et al., 2015: 1398). Shame, guilt, and fear of judgement played a major role in whether participants chose to disclose or not. Women who participated in that study emphasized how the shame and isolation that often accompanied a substance use disorder were amplified by the pregnancy and served to reinforce secrecy and a reluctance to share their substance misuse with providers (Paris et al., 2020: 1399). Ultimately, it was a concern for the welfare of their child and the realization that they needed support to be successful in their recovery attempts and parenting role that led some of them to disclose their problematic substance use (Paris et al., 2015: 1401).

It appears that women with a stigmatized identity are more likely than men to use a support seeking coping strategy, and emotional support may help them seek help (Xiao et al., 2018; Wahto & Swift, 2016; Addis & Mahalik, 2003). However, even if women are generally more likely than men to cope by seeking support, individuals with greater social support networks, regardless of gender, are more likely to engage in various coping strategies, such as acceptance, seeking support, taking direct action, or disengagement (Xiao et al, 2018: 27).

Obviously, gender plays a significant role in how individuals cope with various stigmas and whether they disclose a concealable stigma, as societal expectations and cultural norms influence coping strategies. We will turn now to the specific question of how gender may affect help-seeking behaviour.

Gender and Help-Seeking Behaviour

Stigma is of course only one of the many factors that affect help-seeking behaviour, including gender, culture, religious commitment, or ethnicity (Brenner et al., 2018). Gender, especially, also seems to exert a significant influence on people's help-seeking behaviour, often dictating whether and how individuals seek assistance for the social, physical, mental, or emotional challenges they encounter.

Masculinity itself has been identified as a barrier to seeking help (Heath et al., 2017; McKenzie et al., 2022). Research showed that, on average, men hold more negative attitudes toward psychological help seeking than women. Masculine norms are associated to self-stigma which, in turn, impacts attitudes toward counseling (Hammer, Vogel & Heimerdinger-Edwards, 2013). As a rule, higher levels of gender-role conflict, social stigma, and self-stigma are associated with more negative attitudes toward psychological help seeking (Whato & Swift, 2016).

Women are generally more likely to seek help, particularly for mental health or emotional issues, as societal norms tend to permit and even encourage them to express vulnerability and prioritize self-care (Brenner et al., 2018). However, they may hesitate when seeking help conflicts with caregiving roles or societal expectations. On the other hand, men are less likely to seek help due to cultural norms that associate masculinity with self-reliance, toughness, and emotional suppression. This reluctance can lead to delayed treatment and poorer outcomes, especially for mental health. For non-binary and transgender individuals, the fear of stigma, discrimination, or encountering uninformed professionals often discourages help-seeking. Gendered expectations shape not only whether one feels comfortable seeking help but also the types of support considered socially acceptable, thus perpetuating barriers to effective care.

A study by Brenner and her colleagues (2018) revealed a significant three-way interaction between gender, religious commitment and self-stigma toward seeking psychological help and in determining help-seeking attitudes. The study revealed that self-stigma predicted worse help-seeking attitudes and that men held worse attitudes towards seeking psychological help than women. Men who were connected to their religious beliefs exhibited heightened adherence to traditional masculine standards, thus experiencing feelings of shame upon any deviation from these norms (Brenner et al., 2018).

In the mental health field, for instance, male and female patients respond differently to the anticipated negative impact of a diagnosis and the anticipated stigma. Men and women seem to deal differently with the shame associated with a stigma, and that affects their help-seeking behaviour (Pattyn, Verhaeghe & Bracke, 2015). In fact. men's negative attitudes toward seeking help and the structured social norms that are reconstructed in interactions have been used to explain the gender gap in mental health services (Pattyn, Verhaeghe & Bracke, 2015).

When it comes to men's attitudes towards help-seeking, one often hears jokes about men's unwillingness to seek help, such as asking for directions when lost. While it may be common practice to make light of this stereotypical unwillingness to seek help when needed, it can have serious consequences, particularly where one's health is concerned (Addis & Mahalik, 2003: 6). To understand men's help-seeking behaviour one needs to consider how both the socialization and the societal construction of masculinity interact with the social dynamics of offering and receiving help (Addis & Mahalik, 2003). Psychologists have highlighted the important role that social circles and their accompanying norms play in men's lives and their willingness to seek help (Addis et al., 2003). Linking up with supportive social circles that offer a judgement-free and supportive safe space is critical not only to encourage help-seeking behaviours but also normalizing them.

There have been many studies on the role that gender plays, together with the related cultural expectations and differential access to resources, in shaping help-seeking behaviour, including influence from societal norms, cultural expectations, and access to resources. For example, a study of gender differences in felt stigma and barriers to help-seeking for gambling problems (Baxter et al., 2016) found that both men and women experienced shame about the financial problems that resulted from gambling and that the shame and fear of judgment had an impact on the willingness to seek help. Other barriers to help-seeking were also mentioned: men mentioned the addictive nature of gambling as the next highest barrier to seeking help, and women reported several other barriers including having to admit to being drawn in by the "bells and whistles", feelings of importance in the venue, denial of addiction; feelings of shame as a result of dishonesty were their next highest barriers to help-seeking (Baxter et al., 2016: 6).

Another study examined how gender, religious commitment, and self-stigma impacted help-seeking for mental health issues and found that overall, men had worse help-seeking attitudes than women, whether they had low or high self-stigma, potentially resulting from societal expectations of "stoicism and self-sufficiency" in men (Brenner et al, 2018: 583). A study on help-seeking patterns and attitudes to treatment among men who had attempted suicide, revealed their reluctance to disclose distress and negative attitudes to seeking professional help (Cleary, 2017).

In summary, gender significantly influences help-seeking behaviour, with women generally more open to seeking support and men often hindered by societal expectations around stoicism and independence. Addressing these disparities requires fostering gender-inclusive, stigma-free environments that normalize help-seeking for all individuals, challenge harmful norms, and provide equitable access to tailored support.

Gender and Access to Treatment

Gender also plays a significant role in access to treatment and support, as societal norms and stereotypes often create different barriers for men, women, and gender-diverse individuals. Women may face barriers such as being dismissed by healthcare providers who sometimes attribute their symptoms to stress or emotional instability. Additionally, caregiving responsibilities can limit their time and means to seek treatment. Agterberg (2018) suggested that women face more specific barriers related to their family responsibilities, relationships, and mental health, which not only discourage them, but undermine their ability to access needed supports and services. Additionally, choosing to access treatment for problematic substance use means first disclosing that there is a problem, and women are often unwilling to disclose out of fear of losing custody of their children (Agterberg, 2018).

Gender significantly influences access to treatment and support for various stigmatized conditions. Barriers to treatment differ for men and women, as they are shaped by societal expectations and healthcare system biases. A study on the impacts of mental health stigma found that women who were young, unemployed, single, living in rural areas, or had lower levels of education and lower socioeconomic status, faced higher levels of mental health related stigma (Sayed et al., 2021). Women who face the compounded stigmas associated with lower educational levels and socioeconomic status or with being a woman, young, or unemployed expectably experience greater barriers in accessing the support they need.

Women's Desistance from Crime and Social Reintegration

Here, we stop to consider how criminalized and marginalized women experience stigma and face negative judgements of value and respectability. According to Barr and Rutter (2022), criminalized women are especially stigmatized for not living up to the patriarchal expectations of what it is to be a "good woman". The assumptions surrounding traditional gendered norms also result in criminalized women experiencing higher levels of social stigmatisation. Involvement in crime may come at a higher cost for women in terms of ostracization and social exclusion (Estrada & Nilsson, 2012).

Barr and Rutter (2022: 79) found that the overarching theme reported by women was in relation to their experiences of stigma and shaped by "patriarchal and neoliberal constructions of the good woman", which affects their desistance from criminality and furthers their experiences of harm. They also noted that male focused literature on desistance often placed the burden of male desistance on female partners, furthering the burden of women and emphasizing their stereotypical role as a caregiver and nurturer (Barr & Rutter, 2022).

Criminalized women experience intense stigmatization and frequently internalized that stigma (Barr, 2023; Carlton & Seagrave, 2011; Fredrikson & Gålnander, 2020, Rutter & Barr, 2021; Sharpe, 2024; Stone, 2016; Stone et al., 2018). Grace (2022) referred to women's experiences of extreme anxiety as they seek to avoid disclosure of their criminal past and the anticipated stigma and negative consequences resulting from such disclosure. Moreover, women with a criminal past face major barriers to moral legitimation, social acceptance, and social reintegration (Gålnander, 2020). These barriers often leave those women feeling hopeless (Barr & Rutter, 2022).

Research has shown that stigma, shame and guilt have a disproportionately negative impact on criminalized women (Masson & Österman 2017; Sharpe, 2015; 2024; Stone, 2016), perhaps more so than for men (De Boeck et al., 2018). Women associated with a criminal lifestyle are subject to multidimensional stigmas stemming from criminal conviction, drug use, and gendered expectations (Stone, 2016; Gålnander, 2020). Such multidimensional stigmas can be difficult to overcome when attempting desistance from crime and striving to (re)connect with conventional society. These multidimensional stigmas are often internalized or embodied as part of the women's personal identity, thus complicating their social inclusion or reintegration (Gålnander, 2020; Lander 2015).

It is important to pay attention to gendered differences in how women experience and manage the stigma of criminalization, for example while seeking employment. Gender significantly influences women's desistance from crime and social reintegration, with societal expectations and gendered experiences shaping their paths to rehabilitation. Consistent with the identity theory of desistance, narratives from drug-involved adult women involved in the sex trade and entrenched in the criminal justice system reveal the cognitive transformations that began when they envisioned their "feared self" (e.g., dying alone on the street) (Bachman et al., 2019).

In summary, women who have been involved in criminal activities often face greater stigmatization and fewer reintegration opportunities compared to men. They are judged not only for their criminal past but also for deviating from traditional feminine expectations and roles. This dual stigma can make it harder for women to find support or employment, which are both critical to a successful reintegration. Women may also face unique challenges such as caregiving responsibilities or histories of trauma, which can impair their ability to avoid criminal behaviour or rebuild their lives. Finally, one must recognize and address other intersectional challenges. For instance, because of compounded stigmas, Black or Indigenous women face even greater social reintegration challenges.

6

Coping with Stigma

People cope with stigma as well as they can. The goal of a stigma-informed approach is obviously not to correct people. But opportunities may present themselves to help people better understand how they are affected by stigma and how they typically cope with it. With a little help and gentle encouragement, they may find it useful to reflect on their response to stigma and whether they would wish to change it. They may even signal a desire to talk about their experience or display some healthy curiosity about how others face situations similar to theirs.

Many of the people we interviewed for this study had given a lot of thought to why people react the way they do to stigmatized individuals. One of them, reflecting on his own attitude, shared the following:

"Let me give you an example. Years ago, I watched a show where an actor was playing the role of a very bad man, he was dressed in green. Later, I saw him in a sitcom playing the role of a nice man, but I couldn't get the picture of him in green out of my head. The image was stuck in my head."

In the words of an individual with a serious criminal record:

"You have to manage it (the stigma). If necessary, you can get away from people. You have to choose the people you hang out with. Maybe move to another place."

In Chapter 6, we will be introducing suggestions about how one may provide feedback, support and practical assistance to help individuals manage and cope with stigma. However, in the present chapter we want to focus on how people approach stigma differently, how they cope with it, decide whether to disclose a concealable stigma, and on the main kinds of stigma management strategies they generally resort to. We will do so by presenting what the people we consulted shared with us and note some of the relevant studies on stigma management. Some of the stigma management strategies we will examine have already been mentioned in previous chapters.

The variety of coping strategies people devise to deal with stigma is surprising. Some of these strategies are better than others, and some are unfortunately toxic and profoundly debilitating. It is therefore possible to talk about adaptive as opposed to maladaptive coping strategies. For example, humour can either be used to resist a stigma and challenge stereotypes or in a self-deprecating way that betrays an acceptance or internalization of that stigma. In the following sections we try to organize and synthesize some of that knowledge.

Before moving forward, should we perhaps stop for a moment and ask ourselves whether it would not be better to focus our efforts on eliminating social stigmas and educating people instead of helping those who suffer from them. The answer is obviously that we should do both, even if the focus of this book is on the latter. There is obviously a need for advocacy, awareness raising and education to combat various stigmas, especially in the health, public safety, and support services sectors. At the very least, professionals working in those sectors must be aware of these stigmas and avoid doing anything that perpetuates them. Training people is essential to confront biases and stereotypes, but system change is also necessary to provide a foundation for anti-stigma activities (Foster & Doksum, 2019).

Stigma Management Approaches and Coping Strategies

Stigmatized individuals are not passive recipients of stigmas and prejudice. Neither do they necessarily subscribe to a stigma or internalize it. Many, in fact, find ways to manage the stigma they are facing, reframe or resist it (Hatzenbuehler, Phelan & Link, 2013). They learn, either by trial and error or from others, how to manage the tensions resulting from the judgement or anticipated judgement of others. They also learn how to manage the information they convey in various social interactions in relation to normative expectations of conduct and character. Stigmatized individuals and people who anticipate stigma use various stigma management strategies to try to "pass", avoid shame or embarrassment, or gain acceptance. Moreover, these strategies are not static. They evolve over time together with people's experience of stigma and their adeptness at coping with it.

As someone we interviewed put it:

> *"Sometimes, it all depends on how you hold yourself, how you present yourself. You learn that."*

Distancing oneself physically and mentally from a stigmatized group can be a response to stigma. For example, someone explained how her attitude towards homeless people had changed negatively after she herself had to live in a homeless camp:

> *"When I had a job and I was doing well, I used to feel bad about the homeless people. Sometimes I would try to help. I was feeling a little guilty because I was doing well. Now that I have lived with them for some time, I don't feel guilty anymore. The majority of them are just scoundrels. They are there because of what they did or because they want to be there."*

Research has identified diverse stigma management styles and different approaches to stigma management. Link and colleagues (2004) identified five approaches or *coping orientations*: secrecy, withdrawal, educating, challenging, and distancing. Another interesting categorization distinguishes between reactive and proactive coping approaches. For example, researchers discerned a variety of stigma management strategies with respect to the HIV/AIDS stigma (Siegel, Lune & Meyer (1998). These strategies were arranged along a continuum from reactive to proactive based on the extent to which they implicitly accept or challenge the social norms and values that underlie the stigmatization of HIV/AIDS.

Reactive stigma coping strategies are defensive postures to avoid or mitigate the impact of stigma but imply acceptance of the social norms and values that underly the stigma, whereas *proactive strategies* challenge the validity of the stigma and imply disavowal and resistance of those social norms and values (Siegel, Lune & Meyer, 1998). Building on that work, LeBel (2008) suggested the following three broad categories:

> "*Reactive* strategies include concealment, avoidance or withdrawal, and selective disclosure (i.e. telling some persons who he or she believes will be supportive). *Intermediate* strategies consist of gradual disclosure, selective affiliation, discrediting one's discreditors, and challenging moral attributions. Finally, *proactive* strategies include pre-emptive disclosure (i.e. telling someone before they find out from someone else), public education, and social activism" (LeBel, 2008: 417).

In terms of their outcomes on people's mental health and wellbeing, it seems that any of these approaches is better than self-stigma or apathy, and that proactive approaches are better than reactive approaches to coping with stigma (LeBel, 2018). Other factors can also mitigate the impact of stigma. For example, strong social bonds and social support may act as a protective factor that mitigates feelings and emotions linked to the stigmatization (LeBel, 2012).

Stigma coping strategies may have a significant impact on an individual's social relationships and access to social support. The stigma management and information control strategies utilized by persons with concealable stigma may partly be guided by their expectations of how others would react upon learning about the stigma (Quinn & Chaudoir, 2009; Quinn & Earnshaw, 2013).

With respect to individual resilience to stigma, we know that self-esteem moderates emotional and behavioural responses to stigma and discrimination (Cihangir, Barreto & Ellemers, 2011). Personality traits may also be mitigating factors. For example, some research suggests that highly optimistic individuals are less troubled by anticipated stigma (Moore, Stuewig & Tangney, 2016). Finally, it also appears that adopting healthy vigilance and coping strategies or protecting against anticipated discrimination by modifying one's behaviour mitigate the stress linked to stigma and discrimination (Himmelstein et al., 2015). And stress, as we know, has consequences for health outcomes.

Self-acceptance is also a huge resilience factor for those who face or anticipate stigma. In fact, it is a near pre-requisite to gaining and feeling acceptance by others, especially by loved ones and significant others. During our group discussions with people living with autism, they often mentioned how they had experienced the formal diagnosis of their condition as a liberating moment. For many of them, the diagnosis, together with a new understanding of autism as the normal result of neurodiversity among humans, became a way to interpret and reinterpret their own behaviour in a positive, self-affirmative and self-compassionate light, as well as a means to make sense of the reaction of others to their behaviour. For some of them, the new self-knowledge helped them explain, at least to themselves, some of their past behaviour as normal attempts to gain social acceptance and to avoid stigma, rejection and exclusion. "Finally, it's okay to be me", one of them said.

Zieva Konvisser interviewed women victims of a wrongful conviction and found that many of them saw that experience as an opportunity to reflect, transform, and grow despite the earlier negative life experiences (Konvisser, 2015). After their release, they struggled to reestablish a sense of independence and control over their lives. "Above all", the researcher concluded, "what kept these women going were hope and the defiant power of the human spirit to make healthy choices and embrace life (Konvisser, 2015: 345).

All that suggests that an individual's resilience can be enhanced by supportive interventions based on empowering people to develop agency and self-efficacy, health locus of control and healthy coping mechanisms. Another aspect of these interventions may involve helping stigmatized individuals deal with the powerful emotions triggered by stigma, such as anger, fear, resentment, discouragement or feelings of helplessness.

Identity Management

Stigma coping may also take place internally, in the form of identity management work. For example, several studies of female sex workers have noted the creation of a "sex worker self" as a form of stigma management strategy (Koken, 2012; Quinn & Earnshaw, 2011, 2013). As the sex work is performed by the "sex worker self", these activities are simultaneously detached from the individual's "authentic" self. The strategy helps construct and maintain boundaries between the personal self while presenting a work self to the clients (Scambler, 2007). That coping mechanism includes both an information control element as well as a psychological aspect, in the form of cognitive reframing (Koken, 2012).

People with a spoiled identity may still try to fit in, develop relationships and function socially. This involves efforts to restore their identity, hide it, transform it, or somehow redeem it. One method identified by Goffman (1963) involves the use of disidentifiers or various behavioural signs meant to challenge the validity of a stigma. These signals are meant to help dissociate the individual from a potentially spoiled identity (Goffman, 1963: 44).

At some point, individuals may try to signal that there has been a change in their situation or how they respond to it. That signaling is sometimes meant to conceal or deceive others, but it is also a means to rebuild relationships with others, reinstate a positive identity and overcome the stigma. In criminology, we are familiar with the ex-prisoner's dilemma trying to prove to others that "they are no longer who they used to be" (Maruna, 2012: 75). How can one effectively signal desistance from crime?

Desistance from crime is increasingly understood as a process of cognitive transformation or change in identity whereby individuals stop identifying as offenders and craft non-offender identities (Farrall, 2019; Lussier et al., 2015). Desistance research emphasizes that offenders identify a future self that aids desistance efforts. Hunter and Farrall (2018) described the role of a "future self" in desistance, outlining how a conception of oneself as a non-offender solidifies intentions to refrain from offending. However, gaining social recognition and acceptance of the new self is not without its challenges.

Some people shared with us how hard they had found it was for them to regain social acceptance:

"These problems stick with you; it is so hard to start over. Very few people are willing to give you a real second chance, a fresh start in your relationship with them".

A young woman living with autism admitted that

"It's hard to find the people who validate and who accept you with no judgment and who are willing to make accommodations. I think all those things are very important."

Several individuals talked to us about trying to fit in and regain social acceptance, learning to trust people again, or convincing others to trust them. Many of them had tried very hard to gain social acceptance, especially after they had made what they thought were sincere efforts to address the perceived reasons behind their stigmatization. They may have been in recovery, have desisted from crime, obtained an official pardon, found regular employment, learned a new language, or even volunteered to help others. Nevertheless, their efforts to avoid further stigmatization were not always immediately rewarded, if ever.

The path to building new relationships and rebuilding trust, connection and friendships is sometimes a winding one. Trust is not regained overnight, and people are typically cautious about extending it to those they have labelled as untrustworthy. One young woman explained:

"One has to build trust; demonstrate to people that they can trust you. It takes time. Maybe you volunteer to help them, or you use humour, or you disclose something personal to them hoping that this can lead to building a relationship."

Others cautioned:

"As you try to reestablish trust with people, they test you sometimes. For example, they will leave something of value on a desk or

counter and see whether you take it, or they may tell you some small thing about themselves and see whether you will be repeating it to others."

"If you want to build or rebuild relationships, you have to let yourself be vulnerable. Sometimes you can't."

"I think one of the things that we (people living with autism) have to do, and this is not easy to do, is to be brave enough to make ourselves vulnerable, because that's what we're doing when we're putting ourselves out there and advocating for ourselves. (...) It's really hard to be that vulnerable knowing that people you know, for lack of a better word, will gang up on you and will bully you."

Anticipated rejection, fear and feelings of vulnerability were common among the people we met for the study. One of them, a woman in her sixties, offered the following thoughts:

"The stigmas make it hard to make friends and bond with people, yet some of us also have trouble setting healthy boundaries with people. There have been lots of studies done on the importance of bonding. Often you have the take the first step even if you feel vulnerable. You may expect the worst from others, but you have to give them a chance. How can they trust you if you are not prepared to trust them?"

Another woman who had been estranged from her husband because of her substance abuse problem had cause to be optimistic:

"Some people let you back in their life if you rebuild trust. My ex-husband now helps me when he can, even after all those years. Perhaps he understands the person that I really am, even if I have made some bad decisions."

Signaling change may take many forms, including behaviours that may perhaps appear nonrational, ranging from altruism to conspicuous consumption to self-harming. As Maruna explained:

"Giving of one's time "selflessly to others, throwing money around, or cutting one's wrists and arms are personally costly behaviors, but the reputational "capital" these behaviors purchase may be worth the price. Traditional "costly signals" of remorse similarly have involved acts of self sacrifice and penitence. An individual demonstrates her contrition through apology and acts of restitution, and these acts are formally recognized through acts and gestures of forgiveness" (Maruna, 2012: 78).

The use of redemption scripts, or narratives, is typically part of the process of restoring a positive social identity. A redemption script may begin as an inner narrative, as part of some cognitive reframing, but it must be convincingly communicated to others to result in some kind of redemption. The scripts themselves can take many forms. For example, one study observed that for some incarcerated women, religion offered redemptive narratives to counter punitive carceral narratives. These narratives shift from "flawed" to "faithful" also prescribed specific forms of conduct (e.g., avoiding fights or sex with other women) (Ellis, 2020).

After incarceration, because they fear becoming discreditable in the eyes of others, as a mother, a friend, a colleague, women are known to engage in various compensatory behaviour. For example, some of them may engage in compensatory parenting (Branigan et al., 2023).

People may or may not forgive and accept the stigmatized individual as a changed person unless the change is manifested in action, for example law abiding, sobriety, honesty (Butler et al., 2023). As we also know, people tend to have different beliefs about the redeemability of offenders or the success of rehabilitation programs; many of them are not easily convinced by redemptive narratives and other forms of desistance signaling.

Avoidance and Withdrawal

People who anticipate stigma sometimes manage the risk of being "found out" by avoiding certain people or situations. They maintain their distance from others, including avoiding invitations, new acquaintances or relationships, limiting the time spent with others, limiting others' access to one's home and the potentially revealing information therein), or disappearing from social media. Such withdrawal from situations in which there is the potential for stigmatization impacts behaviour, social relations and functioning (Moore & Tangney, 2017). It leads to various degrees of social isolation.

Avoidance is indeed a frequent pattern of response to stigma, as is exemplified by the following statements from the people we talked with:

"It is harder to face stigma when it comes from your own family. I have cut all contacts with them. I just don't talk to my parents anymore."

"I haven't seen my family in years. I cut them off from my life. What's the point anyway if they don't accept me?"

"The best way to deal with people who mistreat you because of some stigma is to just leave. You can also avoid them in the future, or avoid certain groups, or places."

"One way to avoid being judged or stigmatized is to hang around with your own crowd. Just avoid the others. Just stay away from those better than thou people; what do they know anyway?"

"I don't hang around with stuffy people. Thinking that they are better than me. I am not ashamed of who I am. I try to do what's right."

"When I found out that I could not go with my friends to the US because of my criminal record, some of them asked me about it. But it was not a big deal. Anyway, I don't hang out with high-brow people who would worry about something like that."

"I keep my mouth shut about my criminal record. It's got a lot to do with the mindset of people. It is very embarrassing when the criminal record comes up."

High school students from a minority ethnic group told us about some of the strategies they use at school to avoid further stigmatization:

"In the school as a whole, it is one thing. We just stick with our own group (cultural). It is in the classroom that it gets more difficult, especially in middle school. There are only one or two of you in the group and you are and feel isolated. There often is verbal abuse

or stupid comments. One day, for example, the teacher asked a few students to choose other students to be part of their team for an exercise. No one chose me; in fact, I was the only one who was not chosen by anyone. When it was my turn to choose a partner for an exercise, no one raise their hand. I went home and cried. I told my mother, but she couldn't do much about it. She tried to console me."

"Some youth in my family want so much to fit in, try so hard to be included, that they follow groups that get them in trouble. They go the wrong way because they do not feel accepted by their family, school, immediate community. That's sad."

Predictably, many of those we met for our study had more or less given up on regaining social acceptance and chosen to isolate themselves.

"People try to take advantage of you. I don't need to talk to anyone, maybe I would like to talk to my children, but that's basically it. Being transgender is not easy. A lot of people look at you with contempt. They don't understand what it is like. They don't want to understand. Period."

One formerly homeless individual explained how she sometimes avoided being associated with other people suffering from the same stigma:

"I was living on the street (in a camp) for a short time, and you felt the judgment of people. They can hurt you. But you find ways to avoid some of that. I used to walk further down the main road, far away from the homeless camp to buy things. That way people don't assume that you are from the camp, because you look a little dishevelled. They probably think 'oh, she just having a bad hair day'."

Some individuals also talked about avoiding confrontation, since the latter only seemed to confirm other people's belief that they should be avoided:

"When people say offensive things to you, my parents always told me 'stop and think, don't react too quickly, there is no point in confronting them'. They will go on thinking whatever they want

to think, you are not going to change their mind by just talking to them."

The same for avoiding hurtful behaviour. A young man living with autism shared the following:

"My response is biting sarcasm and keeping an emotional backpack ready by the door so that, if I have to leave, I leave. Like I don't mean physically leave. I mean if I need to emotionally detach from somebody, it's very easy for me."

Several individuals talked about how they had moved, sometimes frequently, to different areas to avoid stigmatization and get a fresh start among people who did not know them. One man recounted his family's experience as it encountered violent stigmatization and exclusion:

"My family and I once moved to a small Ukrainian/Polish rural community in the Prairies where it quickly became obvious that we were not welcome. They literally ran us out of town. They burned down our house. At the time, I was very angry, I think. Don't get me wrong, you have to understand why they did that. My family was invading their community, and they only wanted their own kind to live there. I have learned to avoid places like that. It's better sometimes to live in places where you can blend in, where people cannot single you out and hate you or despise you because you are different."

Avoidance as a response to anticipated stigma is often accompanied by constant vigilance and self-monitoring in social situation to protect oneself from the loss of status that may accompany the revelation of one's stigmatized identity (Weitzer, 2018). Like trauma victims, stigmatized individuals often adopt a *hypervigilant* stance in their social interactions. This vigilance is one of the mechanisms through which discrimination and stigmatization lead to high levels of stress (Himmelstein & Jackson, 2015), including sleep disorders (Hicken et al., 2013) and nightmares (Youngren et al., 2024).

Additionally, some stigmas are sometimes expressed in micro-interactions, including micro-aggressions, to which people who anticipate stigma are particularly sensitive; their vigilance can be exacerbated by such encounters. We have heard from people who explained that sometimes they did not know for sure that they were being aggressed – especially when the other person denied it – and did not know how to respond. One of them explained:

> *"If you don't respond to it, it continues and sometimes gets worse; if you do, it is held against you and it confirms the stigma."*

Whether a stigmatized person chooses to withdraw from certain social interactions or not, the threat of social exclusion, discrimination and isolation by others is still looming. Either way, anticipated stigma creates inequality, undermines trust, and reduces opportunities for positive interpersonal interactions. Through these social processes, stigma interferes with the reconstruction of social capital, including bonding, bridging, and linking social capital. Ironically, social capital is one resource that could mitigate the effects of stigma (McGrath et al., 2013). Social capital accrual and social bonding processes can both act to ameliorate social exclusion (McGrath et al., 2013). Furthermore, social capital, particularly reciprocal cooperation and trust in the community, are possibly associated with lower stigma (Kido et al., 2012).

Most of the people we consulted for our study had very few people with whom they interacted on a regular basis, often no more than one or two outside their immediate family, sometimes none. Often, the very few friends they had were other individuals facing a similar stigma or exclusion. It was clear that some of them, because of their circumstances and the challenges they had faced over the years, had seen their own personal social world shrink down to almost nothing. In many instances, they had very few contacts with family members and many of them were estranged completely or almost from their family. One older man who had not had any contact with his family for many years, following a criminal conviction and imprisonment, said:

> *"I could contact my children, but I don't want to show up empty handed. I have always looked after them and provided them with*

everything they needed. I know that they don't necessarily expect me to give them things, but it is important for me."

For some people, avoiding stigmatization means generally avoiding social contacts. For example, a forty-year-old woman with a drinking problem explained:

"I am not a very social person. At home, I was fine, although I might have gotten a little edgy or mean. Besides my husband and my mother-in-law who lives with us, no one knew about my problem. I was not hiding it; it was just that people would not get to see me drunk."

Another woman of the same age group said:

"I know what isolation is because of physical health issues I have had, including obesity. (...) I knew I needed to lose a lot of weight. I was avoiding people. I did not want people to see me. I had never experienced that before."

Some people had moved to a different location, often to avoid stigmatization, and that had hampered their social and family relationships. Some individuals confided during our discussions that they had consciously avoided striking new relationships to avoid further disappointment or rejection.

One woman who had been trying to cope with drug addiction explained her attitudes towards new social relationships as follows:

"I am a strong independent person. I have no friends. I don't need friends. Maybe I wouldn't mind a few friends, but I don't like sharing personal things with people. People have hurt me; you could say that they did not respect my boundaries. I need to protect myself. I don't want people to come too close to me."

Another woman shared with us how she preferred being alone:

"In fact, I prefer being alone. I don't need a lot of people looking into my own business. One or two people that I can trust is all I need."

A woman who participated in one of our group discussions suggested: "A lot of it is about people not trusting you. People have a lot of trouble trusting others, especially those who do not fit the mold." All the other participants agreed with her statement.

Obviously, none of these avoidance and withdrawal responses to anticipated stigma help individuals engage in a productive therapeutic relationship. Ultimately, the avoidance response to anticipated stigma may inadvertently close people off from potential sources of social support (Koken, 2012). This may have implications, for example, for offenders re-entering the community, possibly hindering community integration and encouraging maladaptive behaviour post-release.

Information Control

As we have seen repeatedly in previous chapters, individuals with a concealable stigma often fear being demonized for breaking social norms and seek to avoid disclosure and the negative reaction of others. For one who faces or anticipates stigma, the issue is not only one of managing the tension generated during social contacts, but also a matter of managing information about one's failings (Goffman, 1963). We must try to understand how stigmatized persons manage or cope with discreditable information about them. Some of it has to do with managing *stigma symbols*, or "signs which are especially effective in drawing attention to a debasing identity" (Goffman, 1963: 43-44). Some of it is also about hiding or disguising one's emotions.

Information control techniques are commonly used by individuals with a secret or concealable defect to present themselves in everyday life and hide crucial information about themselves (Goffman, 1959, 1963). *Communication and information control strategies* are used to dissimulate the situation. They avoid communicating verbally or otherwise signaling or sharing any information that might lead to stigmatization. Stigmatized individuals guard their secret using many common techniques to manage crucial information about themselves (Tally & Littlefield, 2014). For example, they may develop a cover story, avoid certain topics and redirect questions, or simply avoid certain conversations or situations altogether. They learn to signal "all's good here", "nothing to worry about".

As we will see, there are many such techniques and, for those anticipating stigma, the risk of being discovered is often a significant source of stress, anxiety and mental health issues (Quinn & Chaudoir, 2009; Quinn & Earnshaw, 2011; 2013; Koken, 2012; Grace, 2022). Understanding how these concealable stigmatized identities affect psychological well-being is critical to designing effective support interventions.

In the mental health sector, for example, *masking* (or camouflaging) refers to when people hide or supress symptoms, behaviour, and difficulties they are experiencing. It may happen consciously or not, intentionally or not. People mask for different reasons. Victims of intimate partner violence, for example, are often prone to hide or mask signs of physical injuries. Masking is also considered a typical neurodiverse behaviour, particularly among people living with autism or ADHD. In fact, people with various diagnosis mask for various reasons, often to protect themselves or be accepted by others. Unfortunately, masking is very often accompanied by costly personal consequences and, although sometimes necessary, it is not typically a very healthy coping strategy.

In some situations, stigmatized individuals may be able to "pass" as non-stigmatized, despite the cognitive and emotional costs of doing so (Koken, 2012). Some people feel freer in an environment where they are mostly in contact with people facing a similar stigma. It alleviates the fear of involuntary disclosure and improves the possibility of mutual support from others (Colombini et al., 2014). Concealment may be more frequent among people who have internalized stigma and, as we saw in Chapter 1, internalized stigma is related to increased depression, stress, and lower psychological wellbeing.

Consider for a moment how criminal labels have become stickier in recent years, with information technology and data-sharing systems making the concealment of a criminal past increasingly difficult (Lageson, 2016; Lageson & Maruna, 2018; Corda & Lageson, 2020). While the power to apply extralegal criminal labels is now in the hands of many, stigma in the form of a digital footprint is arguably more difficult than ever to escape (Lageson & Maruna, 2018). Data are produced by thousands of different criminal justice agencies and records can lie dormant for years before they reemerge on the Internet when a new digital source releases archived data (Lageson, Webster & Sandoval, 2021; Lageson, 2016, 2022).

Clearly, concealing stigmatized aspects of one's identity can be stressful and have negative implications for mental health (Quinn & Earnshaw, 2011, 2013).

Concealment and Disclosure

In the case of concealable stigmas, individuals face choices about whether and how much they may disclose to others, and how and when to do so. However, concealing one's stigmatized status is neither always possible nor desirable. Many of the people we consulted had frequently struggled with these decisions and sometimes had to change their approach to stigma concealment and disclosure.

A young woman who had battled with addiction said that she often offered the following advice to people in recovery:

> *"If you want to have a relationship you must be opened to letting people find out about your past or your problem. Be an open book, be yourself. If you feel the need to share your life, do it without responding to the pressure to hide. People cannot hold things against you when you are open, if they do, at least you know who you are, who they are, and where you stand."*

However, one older individual with a mental illness history wisely remarked:

> *"I am careful about what I share with others. One thing about the truth is that people generally don't want to hear it. I have learned not to voice my opinion and keep to myself. I am naturally shy, and I hate crowds."*

People living with a concealable stigma often talked about the danger of lying about it, explaining that lying is not a good strategy for building trust and gaining people's confidence:

> "You might as well be open. Lying is not a good strategy, although we have to be careful about what and how much we disclose to others."

> "When they find out about your secret, it is worse than if you had told the truth in the first place."

> "I do not lie. I tell people the truth about my past when they ask. However, people sometimes use that against you."

A young woman suffering from a substance use disorder linked self-honesty to being truthful with others:

> "Don't lie about what's going on in your life, to yourself or to others. If you cannot be honest with yourself, how can you expect others to trust you."

A man with a criminal past shared one of his experiences of hiding his criminal record from an employer:

> "One day, I met one of my old bosses on the street. I had not told him about my criminal past, but he suddenly started to yell at me and confront me. He said, 'people like you never change'. He was very confrontational. I had to dig down deep to find it in me to stay calm and not to respond aggressively. Some other people may not be able to do that."

Another man with a serious criminal record who claimed to have completely desisted from crime and turned his life around talk to us about his experience of seeking a romantic relationship:

> "I think that honesty is the best strategy even if it does not work all the time. It is better than hiding the truth or lying and then having to explain later when the person finds out."

Someone else, a man who was under parole supervision, explained that he did not necessarily have a choice to disclose his situation to some people:

> "I am forced to disclose. I have to disclose my involvement in any relationship to my parole officer. That's part of my conditions. If I don't disclose my relationship with people, my parole officer is likely to bring the subject up when she meets them."

Some stigmas are more easily concealable than others, as exemplified by the following experience of a transgender woman:

> "I get more grief because I am trans, than I get for having a criminal record or being a recovering alcoholic. Some things are easier to hide from people than others. Most people don't even know that I have a serious violent criminal record. There is no reason to tell them, and I don't. Even my children don't know that I spent a few years in prison."

Concealing a criminal past, some people explained, is not always easy, in part because of the media and social media:

> "Just Google my name and you will find out a lot about my past, not all of it true. You will not find anything about the person I am today."

> "Talk about stigma. Just type my name on Google and will find out about my crimes. There is a lot of negative stuff on me on the net. It is there forever. It is not going away. So, I have had to learn to live with it. I better disclose whenever necessary because people will find out really quickly anyway. I also never know whether people have already found out about my past or not."

Someone whose past included a conviction for sexual offences said that, because of the media, he was constantly afraid that someone will recognize him and complain about him for whatever reason. He thought that, because of the strong stigma attached to sex offenders, being identified could bring about some very negative or even dangerous reactions.

A young man with a painful history of institutionalization and youth gang experience who was finding his way in the local art community confided that he feared that he may never be able to fit in and be accepted in that community:

> "I suppose I have a bit of an issue with self-confidence. I am still growing up and learning. Initially, I thought I was a walking bomb. Always out of place. I felt super conspicuous, my own self-consciousness made people treat me differently. I was always worried about being judge, being found out. Sometimes, I want to share my background for people to know me. Sometimes, I don't. I don't always know how to convince people who know me that I have changed. I feel so good when people show that they believe in me."

The people we consulted had had varied experiences of disclosure. For example, participants in the Stand Up for Mental Health program (Vancouver) decide what they want to disclose, through humour, in their stand-up comic number. Another fairly unique and daring experience of disclosure is that of a 65-year-old male who had been convicted and imprisoned for sex offences who accepted to be interviewed for a national television program where he talked openly about his crimes. He said to us, somewhat enigmatically, "I learned a lot from that experience." He added:

> "Years ago, I was in a correctional program with a group for sex offenders where we had to do a disclosure exercise. It was hard, but extremely useful. I don't think the program exists anymore (...) Without being big-headed I can say that I am sort of an expert on disclosure."

A few people told us how risky they thought disclosing a hidden stigma could be. One of them said:

> "You really don't know how people will react. Flip a coin. Disclosure is fifty percent effective with people."

Concealment is a dynamic process that may involve people choosing to actively conceal their status while also choosing to disclose these experiences to a select few. Women who engaged in *selective disclosure* regarding sex work reported greater access to social support, while women who concealed their work from most people often reported feeling lonely and socially isolated (Koken, 2012). Similarly, studies have shown that victims of intimate partner violence tend to disclose their situation to at least one person in their informal network, usually a family member or friend, and when the reaction is supportive, it mitigates the detrimental mental health effects of their victimization (Coker et al., 2002; Sylaska & Edwards, 2014).

Individuals with a serious mental illness often practice selective disclosure. Among those, women are more likely than men to disclose their illness and having lower perceived social support is associated with lower likelihood of disclosure (Pahwa et al., 2017). A person's choice to disclose is influenced by the anticipation of non-judgmental support. Among relational factors, social support is significantly linked with disclosure preferences at the individual level (Pahwa et al., 2017).

You may recall the long discussion in Chapter 4 of gender differences in information disclosing and help-seeking behaviour, and our conclusion that women with a stigmatized identity are more likely than men to use a support seeking coping strategy and that emotional support tends to help them disclose their situation and seek assistance.

Also, as we have seen in Chapter 2, a criminal record is a very powerful and sticky stigma, and there is a lot to learn from the disclosure strategies adopted by ex-offenders. Jobseekers with a criminal record are in a real bind about whether to proactively disclose their record or refrain to do so, with either options holding potential negative outcomes.

Researchers have noted that many individuals with criminal justice involvement, although they anticipate rejection, "wholeheartedly endorse preventative telling as a stigma management strategy" (Winnick & Bodkin, 2008: 295). They tend to prefer *preventative disclosure* to withdrawal and secrecy. On average, men do not tend to hide their criminal past, but many of them nonetheless sometimes rely on a secrecy or concealment strategy (Ramakers, 2022).

During our study we encountered several people who had made a conscious choice to altogether avoid disclosure decisions, sometimes on the advice of friends or counsellors, by professing a completely open attitude about revealing their stigmatized status to others: "I'm an open book"; "I don't want to be ashamed of who I am; you decide whether you want to have anything to do with me." A man who had served 18 years in prison explained:

> *"I am an open book. I don't get on a soap box to tell everyone, but I like to people to know about my criminal past and current situation, because it is better if they find out from me than some other way. That way they don't feel that I deceived or betrayed them, and I don't feel that I let them down. I'd sooner that they learn it from me."*

In a Canadian study, full disclosure was men's most popular strategy after release from prison. It enabled them to exert some control over how they were viewed by others and reduced the fear of not knowing if and when their label would be revealed. Over time, most of them opted for conditional disclosure (Ricciardelli & Mooney, 2018). Disassociation from their criminal self could also explain this change in strategy (Ramakers, 2022).

Harding (2003) found that men with a criminal record consciously employed one of three strategies in their job search: no disclosure, full disclosure and conditional disclosure. In the latter case, individuals attempted to prove that they were good employees before disclosing details of their criminal past, thereby trying to prevent their criminal record to overshadow any personal qualities. Most offenders seemed to opt for no disclosure, due to past rejections based on their criminal record (Harding, 2003; Ramakers, 2022).

Those who are under some form of formal supervision after their release knew that they may have less latitude with respect to choosing to conceal or disclose their situation. In some instances, they may be under some instructions to reveal their criminal record to others. However, the stigma associated with being monitored can make it harder to find employment, stable housing, or community support, all of which are crucial to a successful reintegration.

People may selectively share their experience of stigmatization with others either to share with them (stigma-sharing) or test them (stigma-testing). One study showed that satisfactory past disclosure experiences of depression were associated with decisions to disclose to someone close and lower current reports of public stigma (Cipollina, Sanchez & Mikrut, 2022).

There is unfortunately not a lot of information about what is the most satisfying or constructive way of disclosing information about a stigmatized aspect of one's situation. In the case of mental illness, a study of *disclosure directness*, or the degree to which one explicitly discusses a mental illness stigma during a disclosure experience, suggested that directness could lead to more satisfying disclosures (Cipollina, Sanchez & Mikrut, 2024).

Studies on the consequences of disclosure of a concealable stigma are similarly limited. One study suggested that disclosure of an invisible disability can impact the formation of romantic relationships among people with disabilities (Mimoun & Margalit, 2023). Another study considered the impact of both revealing a year of inactivity or a year of inactivity due to former depression when applying for a job. It found that both decreased the probability of getting a job interview (Baert et al., 2016). Similarly, disclosing a need for a disability-related accommodation during a job interview, especially for an invisible disability, was found to negatively affect an individual's employability (Ameri & Kurtzberg, 2022).

Disclosing may have a positive psychological effect, depending on the response one receives following the disclosure. The psychological benefits of the disclosure experience depend on whether the individuals feels supported and accepted after disclosing a concealable stigmatized identity. As Chaudoir and Quinn (2010) explained, positive and supportive disclosure experiences may have long-term psychological benefits, possibly because it may help relieve people's chronic fear of disclosure.

> "Receiving support and positive feedback during the first time a stigmatized identity is disclosed may lead people to experience a greater sense of trust in others and a comfort in disclosing personal information" (Chaudoir & Quinn, 2010:10).

There is also evidence of the potential negative health consequences of disclosing a mental illness (Quinn & Chaudoir, 2009; Quinn & Earnshaw, 2011, 2013). Disclosure of a mental illness may expose individuals to additional discrimination and social disapproval. However, when Corrigan and his colleagues compared coming out to other approaches of controlling self-stigma for serious mental illness, they found people who had disclosed their condition often reported benefits, such as feeling empowered or experiencing lower self-stigma (Corrigan et al., 2010; Corrigan, Kosyluk & Rüsch, 2013).

Resistance

The flip side of self-stigmatization is denial or rejection of the stigma:

"That's not me. (...) I want nothing to do with such a shameful identity."

Some of the people we met during the study resisted the labels they believed others were trying to force upon them:

"When I see that people are judging me or treating me poorly because of who they think I am, I just say something. I don't have to take that kind of shit from anyone. If you don't like it, too bad for you."

"On the street, you have to be tough. You can't let people put you in a box or hurt you. Keep your pugs up."

A middle-aged woman who complained about her family members not respecting her personal boundaries, because they had labeled her as unfit to make her own decisions, explained how she was trying to fight that stigma and regain control over her life:

"I decide what I do, what I eat, what I drink, where I live. It's nobody's business. I want to tell people 'back off', mind your own business. (...) I am tired of people wanting to tell me what to do all the time, telling me that I am not normal, that what I am doing is not healthy for me. My attitude is 'back off', that's my life, my body, my head, my lungs, my stomach."

An older ex-offender who felt he had successfully reintegrated into the community talked about the experience of being unjustly stigmatized. Like others, he talked about showing self restraint in how he reacted to those situations:

> "My criminal record is bad enough without people adding to it things that are not true. It's hard when people stigmatize you and judge you for things that you did not do. There have been a lot of stories about me, including on the internet, that are not true. I also know that my ex-wife told my children some stories that are not true, probably to get the divorce. It takes a lot out of me not to get mad about these false things."

A woman working in the healthcare sector shared with us her one experience of resisting a stigma:

> "At work, people judge my character. I don't let that affect me. It's their choice. That's all they view. I once tried to get people around me to change their attitude. Because I raised the issue, I was moved out of that workplace. People have this idea that you are a bad person. In your situation, these people may have done a lot worst than you did. Some people never change, so forget it, you will not change them."

Stigma resistance is an ongoing, active process of using one's experiences, skills and knowledge to develop a positive identity. Researchers have suggested that resisting stigma can occur at three different levels: personal, peer, and public sigma resistance (Firmin et al., 2017). According to these researchers, resisting stigma at the personal level often appears to be a prerequisite that enables resisting stigma at the peer and public levels. It includes not believing stigma/challenging stigmatizing thoughts, empowering oneself through education, proving stigma wrong, and developing identity apart from mental illness. Stigma resistance at the peer level involves using one's lived experiences to help others, formal peer-service involvement, and support of friends and family with lived experience. Finally, stigma resistance at the public level includes challenging, confronting and questioning stigma, educating others, disclosing one's lived experience and advocating for people with mental illness (Firmin et al., 2017).

It is obviously easier for some people than for others to resist stigma, especially if they are empowered to do so. Greater reflective capacity, greater self-esteem and self-efficacy and fewer endorsements of the negative stereotypes are key factors related to higher levels of stigma resistance (Kao et al., 2017).

A study involving interviews with seventeen people deemed ineligible for criminal record expungement found that emotion displays played a role in stigma resistance (Ispa-Landa & Loeffler, 2016). Individuals challenged stigmatizing definitions of themselves by offering optimistic accounts of their future wellbeing and displayed anger towards the criminal justice system. They reported distress, hopelessness, hurt, anger and anxiety about the future due to their subjection to ongoing stigma (Ispa-Landa & Loeffler, 2016; Ispa-Land, 2019).

Another study examined the stigma resistance strategies of mothers who were claiming social security benefits (Evans, 2022). These mothers denounced the welfare stigma and its implications of incompetent motherhood, the devaluation of caring labour, and the perception that the security benefits are undeserved. However, their individual resistance efforts were curtailed by the power and pervasiveness of the structurally imposed stigma.

Despite tacitly accepting many of the negative views directed at them, many sex workers actively resist the stigma attached to their work. Sallmann (2020: 155) explained that: "although they may not actively try to justify their involvements in prostitution and substance use, they accepted responsibility for their actions but also recognized the social double standards against which they were judged and ultimately found deficient". It has also been suggested that the temporariness of sex work may allow resistance to a potentially stigmatizing identity by positioning sex work explicitly as something one does for a limited period, rather than as a master status or identity (Ham & Gilmour, 2017).

Stigma resistance, in its many forms, appears to be negatively associated with self-stigma and positively associated with social functioning, self-esteem, self-efficacy, hope, and problem-centred coping (Firmin et al., 2016, 2017, 2017a; O'Connor, Yanos & Firmin, 2018).

Seeking Redemption

In addition to what we learned previously about the use of redemptive narratives, some stigmatized individuals make other conscious attempts to regain social acceptance. It is also a form of active stigma resistance. Several people explained to us how they thought that openly apologizing and making amends helped them regain some social acceptance and rebuild trust with others. One individual reflected on something he had seen on television:

Several individuals explained to us how they thought that openly apologizing and making amends helped them regain some social acceptance and rebuild trust with others. One individual reflected on something he had seen on television:

> *"Yesterday, I saw a well-known actor who got in trouble for using the 'N' word. He was on TV explaining how he had come to terms with his outburst, and he apologized for having used the 'N' word. It helped me accept him."*

We heard from several people who had tried to gain social acceptance by volunteering or to reunite with family and friends by offering to help them. One of them thought:

> *"Sometimes, you can offer to help someone, that's a good starting point. You can also try to share something personal with them. You have to give people time to get to know you as a person, to go over the stigma."*

But that strategy does not always bare fruit, as someone's experience appeared to confirm:

> *"Even when I volunteer or try to help others, I find that people don't trust me. The staff (in a support program) sometimes tell me*

to mind my own business. I don't know why people are so suspicious around me. I don't think that it's just me or because I am transitioning."

For some individuals, social acceptance was sought by joining a religious group or finding solace in the belief that God, at least, was accepting them. For some the experience was transformative and deeply soothing. Linking with a faith-based group also opened the possibility of developing new social relationships. One young person told us:

"One has to believe in something bigger that ourselves. I am not religious, but I believe in the Creator. My friend and former roommate introduced me to some Indigenous ceremonies. I made other friends there."

However, for others, the response they had from fellow worshipers was not always what they had hoped for. For example, one woman explained:

"When I was going to church and got baptized, I was working with the children at the church. The ladies were looking down on me. A friend of mine I had just gotten to know a little went to tell people 'I don't know whether you want that person in your home'. I asked her why she was doing that. Later, she apologized to me, and we have been friends ever since. (...) I stopped going to church. I believe in God, and I have my own relationship with him. When you are baptized you start a new life, but they (members of the church) closed the door on me. I cried."

It is interesting to observe how volunteering emerges as a form of resistance against self-stigma among individuals who resiliently continue to seek belonging and purpose (Jordan, 2022). One way of proactively dealing with stigmatization that appears to be successful for some people in recovery, formerly incarcerated persons and persons with mental illness, involves becoming a "professional ex" or peer supporter (LeBel 2008). In general, that coping strategy is based on a desire and commitment to reach back and help other similarly stigmatized people by sharing one's experiences, strength and hope with others who are less far along in recovery and reconnection with mainstream society (McNeill & Maruna 2007). This resistance strategy seems to help stigmatized individuals redeem themselves and the damage caused by previous actions and sometimes mitigates structural barriers to affiliation with the mainstream (McNeill & Maruna 2007; Gâlnander, 2020). It can contribute to desistance from crime. A recent study of the volunteering experiences of 16 women experiencing criminal record stigma showed that criminalized women can take on the volunteer worker identity to provide a positive, alternate personality, contributing to desistance from crime (Barr, 2023).

Help Avoidance

As we saw earlier, coping mechanisms like avoidance and withdrawal negatively affect help seeking behaviour. Avoiding those who can help us is often one of the consequences of self-stigma and shame. Some researchers talk about the *why try?* effect of self-stigma. Self-stigma worsens individuals' sense of worthiness, which in turn affects self-agency, personal capability and results in increased depression (Corrigan et al., 2016; 2019; Yu et al., 2023).

People sometimes do not seek help for fear of being negatively judged or face repercussions such as losing custody of their children (Timko et al., 2016). That fear of stigmatization and rejection prevents many individuals from seeking assistance. A transgender individual who had been sexually assaulted explained:

> *"I was sexually assaulted last week, but I did not tell anyone. I think that the guy just hated me for being a trans. I am not sure why I did not report it. I am sure the police would ridicule me if I did. Maybe I should."*

A woman in her early fifties explained that she had sometimes listened to other people and thought that she perhaps did not deserve to be helped:

> *"I want people to continue thinking that I manage well on my own. That coping part of it perhaps drove me to drink more, the shame of it. I am supposed to be strong and know my limits. Knowing that I don't live up to people's expectations and that I am a failure in everybody's eyes, I thought perhaps that I did not deserve to be helped. But I was wrong, once I started to get help, I found that there were a lot of people willing to help me. My shame had turned into a strength."*

There is a lot of research on the fear of stigmatization as a major deterrent to seeking mental health or substance use treatment (Allen, Copello, & Orford, 2005; Jackson & Shannon, 2012; Cumming et al., 2016; Cunningham et al., 1993; Wu et al., 2011; Agterberg, 2018). Recall also what we saw earlier, in Chapter 4, about the many other factors that affect help-seeking behaviour, including gender, culture, religious commitment, or ethnicity. Gender, especially, seems to exert a significant influence on people's help-seeking behaviour.

Multiple studies have also linked lower levels of adherence to treatment to higher levels of self-stigma. Conversely, lower levels of self-stigma are associated with fewer missed appointments and greater adherence to treatment (Carrara & Ventura, 2018; Conklin, 2021; Batchelder, 2021). Self-stigma can impair the initial decision to seek help, because of isolation and concealment (Lannin et al., 2015; Lannin et al., 2016). Other research has underlined the relevance of the stigma associated with help-seeking itself, particularly in relation to drug treatment programs (Fox, Smith & Vogt, 2018; Cunningham et al., 1993; Lanning, 2015).

As was mentioned in previous chapters, some individuals manage the risk of detection by health personnel, including by lying about their situation or the pain they experience, skipping treatment appointments, or avoiding treatment altogether (Stone, 2015). An anticipated stigmatization is also known to discourage some substance-using mothers from seeking comprehensive medical treatment during their pregnancies (Stone, 2015), to negatively affect service use and therapy adherence by women living with HIV/AID (Colombini et al., 2014), to prevent many people from seeking treatment for alcoholism (Cunningham et al., 1993), or to negatively affect methamphetamine treatment access (Cumming et al., 2016).

Similarly, a study of sex workers' help-seeking behaviour indicated that the sex workers' previous experiences of stigma and discrimination significantly impacted their intentions to seek mental health support in the future (Rayson & Alba, 2019). An experience of stigmatization and discrimination by mental health professionals predicted a lower likelihood of future help-seeking. Like people dealing with mental illness, the sex workers had learned to expect less from healthcare services (Rayson & Alba, 2019).

7

A Stigma-informed Approach

Many of the people we are trying to help and support have a long history of trying to cope with biases, stigmas and discrimination. This influences their ability to seek help and participate fully in a support or treatment program.

We must be attentive to the ways our own biases and stereotypes influence our interventions and perpetuate various stigmas. However, just as it is important to understand how various stereotypes and biases may affect our interventions, it is also important to understand how self-stigma and anticipated stigma may affect the people we are trying to help. Service providers working with people facing or anticipating stigma can fail to recognize the interconnections between their clients' stigmatized circumstances and their behaviour and self-presentation.

We saw in the previous chapter the many ways, not all of them very effective, in which people try to cope with and manage stigma. We also saw how anticipated and self-stigma directly affect whether and how people go about seeking and receiving assistance. Obviously, there is much more that we need to learn about how people tend to cope with various forms of stigmatization and how we might be able to support and help them.

The people who participated in our study often had a disappointing experience of asking for assistance or trying to find a safe space where to disclose their issues. As some of them told us, help is not always forthcoming:

> "People internalize stigma. They go to therapy, support groups, talk amongst themselves. They try to talk about it. It is very hard because here you are and you are trying to reach out for services and then you find out that you have to educate people, the helpers, the public. I don't think that there are any real effective helping mechanisms."

> "Disclosure is a big part of the dilemma and the process. People need a safe space to disclose what they want to disclose, how they want to disclose, and when they want to do it. That is empowering."

> "In our support group, no one is pushed to disclose anything. Most of the people actually want to talk, share their experience. They feel empowered, once they do."

A stigma-informed approach implies that we try to understand how people's stigma coping strategies affect how they relate to others, including those purporting the help them, as well as the context in which the helping interventions take place. It therefore requires that we listen patiently and with openness to the experience they share with us and validate it.

A consequence of self-stigmatization that we have already mentioned is the "why try" effect, in which self-stigma interferes with agency and the active pursuit of life goals. People are dissuaded from pursuing their goals because of diminished self-esteem and self-efficacy. In brief, experiencing stigma can be profoundly disempowering.

Individual resilience is the maintenance of positive adaptation by individuals despite experiences of significant adversity. A stigma-informed approach is essentially about empowering people to cope with stigma in a healthy and self-affirming way and helping them develop resilience. A key to addressing self-stigma is to promote personal empowerment, self-efficacy and agency. Empowerment is, in a sense, the flip side of stigma, involving agency, control, activism, righteous indignation, and optimism.

By facilitating agency and self-efficacy, empowerment can lead to higher self-esteem, better quality of life, greater adherence to treatment, and increased social support. Empowerment and resilience building interventions may take different forms, including stigma reduction, stigma remediation, or counselling and treatment interventions. We explore them in more detail in this chapter.

A stigma-informed approach to helping others applies to every aspect of case management, from outreach activities and intake to aftercare support. It aligns perfectly with a client-centred and client-empowering approach to case management which involves helping clients increase their sense of self-worth and self-efficacy, their autonomy and agency, and their access to opportunities and resources. It also involves helping them restore their power and control over their own life, cope with the social stigmas and exclusion they face, and build on their ability to effect change and achieve their personal goals. In addition to being gender responsive, culturally appropriate, and trauma-informed, it implies that every aspect of every individual or group intervention is:

- Helpful from the clients' own perspective
- Enabling and empowering by building on the clients' strengths and letting them guide themselves and grow in confidence of their own abilities
- Individualized and respectful of the clients' own decisions and personal goals
- Offered in an accessible, timely and flexible manner
- Delivered in a consistent, constant, coherent, coordinated, dependable and sustainable manner.

In practice, effective stigma resistance and resilience building interventions are often based on the experience and contribution of service users – people with experiences – and their involvement in the interventions that are developed and implemented.

Since many of our clients have had recurring experiences of negative stigmatization and discrimination, including sometimes from service providers, they have learned strategies to cope with stigmatization and avoid further rejection. However, these coping strategies and the associated maintenance of multiple identities are accompanied by the need for vigilance, avoidance and isolation, potentially compounding the negative outcomes of anticipating or experiencing stigma and discrimination.

With that in mind, we must take care not to misinterpret a client's non-disclosure, selective disclosure, vigilance, isolation, or conflicting signals. None of those necessarily indicates an unwillingness to fully engage in a program. We must respect the fact that these normal self-protection and risk management strategies allow our clients to mitigate the effects of stigma in their public and personal worlds. We can do so by adopting a respectful and non-judgmental attitude, building rapport, expressing genuine interest and empathy, listening, attending, and communicating honestly with them.

Stigma Reduction

Stigma reduction interventions aim to reduce both the incidence and the burden of stigma (Hartog et al., 2020). First and foremost, the "do no harm" principle applies. Support services and helping interventions should not in any way compound the self-stigma or anticipated stigma already experienced by clients. One practitioner noted:

> *"This highlights for me the importance of a bit of an organized strategy to advocate to organizations so they are aware of the impact of policies which can create feelings of stigma. I think most support organizations don't do enough to understand the barriers they may create for people, or how people feel while moving through a hiring process, so I'm curious about how people can be empowered to bring these concerns forward."*

Numerous studies have revealed how common negative attitudes of professionals towards clients contribute to suboptimal care and support for stigmatized individuals (Van Boekel, 2013; Ford, 2011; Treloar et al., 2021; Carlson et al., 2017). Because of these attitudes, individuals with a stigmatized identity frequently avoid sharing details about their situation with lawyers, doctors, nurses, therapists and other service providers.

Similar experiences are reported by ex-offenders (Schwarz, 2020), sex workers (Treloar et al., 2021), people suffering from mental illness (Ford, 2011) or substance use problems (Carrara, Bobbili & Ventura, 2023), which can affect their access to healthcare and other support services. Also, studies have shown how experiences of weight stigma in a medical environment shape clinical interactions and lead to avoidance of healthcare (Robinson et al., 2024; Ryan, 2024).

Many people who participated in our study mentioned how they thought stigmas had negatively affected the way they were treated by service providers:

"My friend was treated horribly at the local hospital once the ER staff realized that he had been using drugs."

"You know you are going to be treated differently than other people (talking about healthcare services providers). That's demeaning. It makes me feel angry, but I would rather not put up with that."

"I saw how they (hospital staff) treated someone they thought had a mental health problem. It was horrible the way they treated him. I was embarrassed for them."

"When I moved here, I had to get a new doctor and during my first meeting with him, I was honest about my past, about my addiction and about being clean for about seven years. The moment I told him that, his whole demeanour and physical appearance changed. It made me feel so uneasy. I got the cold shoulder treatment. (...) He just wanted to get out of the room as soon as he could. I did not want to be his patient. I left. In the past all my other doctors had been very compassionate and respectful; not him."

"The stigma about drugs and all the prejudice always makes it doubly hard to get help. People immediately judge you, blame you. After a while, you feel shame."

Some of them told us how stigmas continue to operate even within an organization designed to help them:

"The people here (in a help centre) take great care to distance themselves from you, to emphasize that they are not like you. I am not sure they are aware that they are doing that. It is difficult to talk or open-up to someone who does not understand you, has no idea of what you are going through. For me, it is a boundary issue."

"Workers here (a residential support centre) do it too. They judge you and treat you like you are a lesser human being. How dare they? They would be right here with me if they had not benefited from their parents and their nice little life. The new staff is the worst, they have no idea of what it is like to struggle like we do – they had a nice comfortable little life, and they are often too young. They have very little life experience. They don't understand what we are going through, how could they?"

"I am tired of people, including the staff there (a treatment facility), who were constantly trying to belittle me. I don't think that they really wanted to be helpful. For them, most of them, it is just a job and a paycheque. I keep reminding myself not to expect too much from them."

At the same time, many individuals shared with us how the support they had received from staff from various helping organizations had made a real difference in their life. One of them said:

"The staff at the residence are so compassionate. They act like it is their calling, they look like they are not working but doing what feels good for them. They don't judge you."

Seeking help was difficult for many of the people we talked to. Some of them who had internalized stigmas wondered whether they deserved being helped. Many of them felt that, after disappointing so many people who had tried to help them, they no longer had any right to expect anyone to want to help them. For example, two young men shared the following with us:

"I feel uncomfortable asking for help. My family does not help. I used to ask my family members for help, but they never tried to help me. After a while you think 'what's the bloody point'. If my own family is not prepared to help me, why would other people try to help me?"

"I don't ask for help. I don't want to burden anybody else with my problems. It is important to me to be self-sufficient. I admire people who are self-sufficient. I used to be able to look after myself without any help; I can do it again."

Several individuals expressed a need for professional support and guidance, sometimes referring specifically to the need for counselling. However, many of them had had negative experiences with professional counsellors and were doubtful about their ability to help them. For example, we heard comments such as the following from many individuals who had experienced various stigmas because of mental health or substance use issues:

"God knows I could use the help of a counsellor right now; a good one. Some of them just do it to be paid, they don't care about you. Some of them have no idea of what they are doing. I don't even think that they can understand what you are going through. I don't know, maybe they could if they really tried."

"My experience with various counsellors has been mostly bad. They tell you to trust them, open-up, but once they hear your sob story, they drop you or lose interest."

"One of them (a counsellor) insisted that I should sort my shit out before coming to her. But that's exactly why I had come to see her in the first place, to help me get things sorted out."

"Counselling is so expensive. People should be able to access it when they need it. Not just counselling, but good counselling. I had access to two counsellors through an employment assistance program. The first one kept repeating that there was no reason for me to feel paralyzed: 'you're beautiful, you're intelligent, you were good at work, just get out there, and then she asked me if I wanted her to

introduce me to her son for a date. I asked for another counsellor. That one got me to help him understand a particular software on his computer, then he offered to purchase season tickets for the two of us for the Vancouver Symphony, suggesting that we could start dating. I did not continue with him."

In a drop-in centre for homeless people, an individual was actively seeking to convince others that they should just give up seeking the help of a counsellor: "There is no point. You'll just waste your time or even get hurt."

One young man recently released from a youth justice institution explained that he did not receive any help:

"I had to do it by myself, find value in myself. It's nice to have support, but I am not dependent on others."

Most of the people we consulted relayed how difficult it had been for them to find the support they needed. A woman in the process of applying for a criminal record suspension and suing a former employer for discriminating practices explained:

"I needed to break those shackles that had been holding me back. For the longest time there was no one to help. I really felt alone. The way I am, I am not going to ask for help. Now I realize how helpful people can be if I let them. My new lawyer helped me understand that. (...) Later, as I was searching for a support group, I thought 'I cannot be the only one facing that kind of situation'. There were none. All that just made me feel even more isolated. It takes a lot of effort to try to explain to people what you are going through. There is a lot of ignorance out there. After a while, it is easier to give up trying."

Some people had found great support in a program they had participated in. For example, the Vancouver-based *Stand Up for Mental Health* program, based on humor and training as a stand-up comic, seems to have a beneficial effect on those who chose to participate in it. The program is a strength-based way to fight with stigma. It is a confidence builder, and it helps people acquire a sense of agency. Participants had typically tried other programs that did not work for them. Unlike their experience with other programs, participants felt pride instead of shame:

> "Wow, I told everyone about the worst things I can do, and they are applauding. Maybe I am not so bad after all."

Because self-stigma stems from the negative reactions or anticipated reactions of others, the most powerful weapon against it is to facilitate more positive and supportive attitudes towards people it affects. Healthcare organizations and other service providers have relied on various awareness raising and education-based initiatives, including contact-based training, to reduce biased attitudes and stigmatization within their own culture and practices (Latkin et al., 2013; Livingston et al., 2012; Hackler, Cornish & Vogel, 2016). However, these initiatives are not always enough to effectively reduce stigma within an organization (Hamilton, Coleman & Krendl, 2023). The stigma reduction literature argues for approaches involving targeted, local, credible and continuous contact with stigmatized persons, as well as interaction strategies that can be used by stigmatized persons to deflect biases (Bos et al., 2013; Hamilton, Coleman & Krendl, 2023; Hackler, Cornish & Vogel, 2016).

There are also initiatives that are meant to reduce the stigmatization resulting from crime for both offenders and victims, including mediation, facilitated dialogue, and restorative justice. Shame is often a dominant feeling for people who have internalized powerful social stigmas, and feeling ashamed correlates with poor self-esteem, negative self-concept, and multiple mental health issues. Research also suggests that experiencing high levels of shame increases the risk for a range of high-risk behaviours, including substance use, self-harm, and suicidal ideation (Tilghman-Osborne, 2008). The assumption is that mediation and restorative justice interventions can replace stigmatizing shaming, which disempowers, marginalizes and labels offenders, with reintegrative shaming (Braithwaite, 1989, 1996).

Stigma Remediation

There are several examples of proven stigma remediation initiatives. There are least two prominent approaches for self-stigma reduction: (1) interventions that attempt to alter the stigmatizing beliefs and attitudes of the individual, and (2) interventions that enhance skills for coping with self-stigma through improvements in self-esteem, empowerment, and help-seeking behaviour (Mittal et al., 2012; Hing & Russel, 2017).

Challenging Self-stigma

People often face compounded stigma. They may or may not fully understand the role and impacts that stigma and self-stigma have in their life. For many of them, it is a sensitive and difficult matter to address, one charged with many deep and unbearable emotions. They are often looking, consciously or not, for empathic emotional support. We know, for example, that individuals who feel a higher level of emotional support are more likely to take advantage of available support resources (Xiao et al., 2018; Wahto & Swift, 2016; Addis & Mahalik, 2003). Social support, whether emotional, functional or informational, is significantly correlated with all effective stigma management approaches (Xiao et al., 2018). Providing practical support – e.g., safety planning, accompanying someone through their contacts with the healthcare and criminal justice systems – offers a practical way to express empathy, solidarity and build rapport.

Individuals with higher levels of social support are apparently more likely to use various healthy coping strategies and resist isolation. Positive relationships and solidarity can inform stigma resistance initiatives (Barr & Rutter, 2022). Helping individuals mobilize social support and develop rewarding social interactions can help them counter the debilitating effects of self-stigma.

Positive relationships which help challenge feelings of shame and stigmatization often play an important role in people's desistance from crime or their recovery from substance use and mental illness (Rutter & Barr, 2018; Celinska, 2000). Participation in self-management support group activities can also be encouraged. People can sometimes negotiate a worthy identity in such groups and thus find the means to fight self stigmatization and reduce its effects (Bossy et al., 2017).

Encouraging resistance to stigma through positive relationships and solidarity may also be an important consideration for practice (Rutter & Barr, 2022). Interventions may include motivational interviewing, evidencing understanding, and communicating positive stories of people facing similar situations (Livingston et al., 2012).

It is equally possible to reduce the effects of self-stigma by helping someone develop self confidence and trust and helping them selectively disclose their stigmatized situation, as the need arises, to colleagues, neighbours, and others around them. That may impact their chronic fear of disclosure (Corrigan, Kosyluk & Rüsch, 2013).

Providing a safe context for disclosure and providing support and positive feedback can improve self-esteem and self-confidence and foster a greater sense of trust in others and comfort in sharing personal information (Chaudoir & Quinn, 2010). Positive and supportive disclosure experiences, particularly about a concealable stigma, have long-term psychological benefits (Chaudoir & Quinn, 2010; Corrigan, Kosyluk & Rüsch, 2013).

Even humour, as was mentioned earlier, can be part of a stigma remediation strategy. It can prove to be a powerful tool for coping with enacted, anticipated stigma, and even self-stigma.

Stigma Management and Coping Skills

Helping people develop an awareness of how they choose to cope with stigma can be very helpful to them. Helping them reflect on what they disclose or fail to disclose to others, what they are signalling during everyday interactions, including inadvertent or unconscious signaling, and how they avoid contacts and isolate themselves can help them develop self-confidence and self-efficacy. To help them develop a form of mindfulness, one may ask: How do you present yourself in everyday interactions with others? What are you signalling to others in everyday life, consciously or unconsciously? What are you signaling through the emotions you express?

We can think of the young street-attached girl who dresses like a boy and does not wash herself to protect herself against unwanted sexual advances, or the boy with tight fists who walks the same streets constantly trying to signal "don't mess with me." Many of these behaviours are understandable defensive postures, but the same defensive stance is also what prevents someone to engage in more positive and supportive relationships.

Self-compassion

Developing self-acceptance and self-compassion are to some extent prerequisites to gaining and feeling social acceptance, or at the very least acceptance from significant others. Self-soothing behaviour, self validation and self-compassion may protect against stigma-related poor mental health outcomes (Helminen et al., 2023).

Self-validation is a self-compassionate practice in which people are taught to consider and name the ways in which their emotions make sense. Self-validation requires a mindful stance toward emotions and the use of nonjudgmental language toward the self. Self-validation is not a state or goal that can be achieved but rather a skill that must be developed and practiced, with each new emotion presenting a new opportunity to practice it.

Teaching and modeling self-compassionate actions – and mindfulness – may be helpful because stigma, discrimination and rejection interfere with learning how to treat oneself compassionately (Cardona, Cohen & Feinstein, 2023; Sánchez, 2023). A self-affirmation intervention wherein participants reflect on an important personal characteristic may also help (Lannin et al., 2013). In the end, self-compassion is most effectively taught as a continual process, "building it like a muscle" (Cardona, Cohen & Feinstein, 2023: 41).

According to Neff (2003), self-compassion is thought to involve three main aspects: self kindness (i.e., the ability to treat oneself with understanding rather than criticism in moments of pain or struggle); common humanity (i.e., a sense of connection to the larger human experience rather than feeling separate or isolated); and mindfulness (i.e., the ability to attend to one's emotions with awareness and without overidentification).

The self-compassionate action of allowing and accepting the emotions that arise, such as anger at being mistreated or sadness about losing social connections, is essential (Cardona, Cohen & Feinstein, 2023). It involves addressing the emotions associated with stigma, especially internalized stigma (e.g., shame, anger, sadness) and understanding how these emotions relate to their social withdrawal and isolation as well as their attitude towards seeking assistance. Cardona, Cohen and Feinstein (2023) explained how stigma resistance itself can be a self-compassionate response to stigma:

> "If shame is telling this client that their current social group is rejecting them, and the emotion of shame does fit the facts (i.e., the social group actually is rejecting or excluding them), it is understandable that the client's impulse might be to conceal their identities; this response attempts to protect them from rejection or other harm, especially if leaving the group is not an option. Alternatively, fact-fitting and inherently self-compassionate responses may be to advocate for oneself with the goal of trying to change the norms of the social group, or to leave the social group to find an affirming one" (Cardona, Cohen & Feinstein, 2023: 41).

Some people have trouble practicing self compassion. They seem to struggle to show themselves compassion even with encouragement and practice (Cardona, Cohen & Feinstein, 2023). Some of them may have difficulties with self-compassion that are related to histories of trauma and traumatic invalidation (Cardona, Madigan & Sauer-Zavala, 2022). It is important, therefore to remind ourselves that, for some people, practicing self-compassion can be incredibly difficult, as it may include experiencing vulnerability, fear, sadness, grief, and other emotions they are precisely trying to avoid.

As already mentioned, masculinity itself can be a barrier to seeking help. However, self-compassion can play a role in the relationship between masculine norm adherence and help-seeking stigma and the risks associated with self-disclosing to a counselor. Self-compassion, it would seem, serves as a protective factor in the relationship between overall masculine norm adherence and each of these barriers (Heath et al., 2017).

Counselling Interventions

According to the Dictionary of Psychology of the American Psychological Association, resilience is:

> "The process and outcome of successfully adapting to difficult or challenging life experiences, especially through mental, emotional, and behavioral flexibility and adjustment to external and internal demands. Several factors contribute to how well people adapt to adversities, predominant among them (a) the ways in which individuals view and engage with the world, (b) the availability and quality of social resources, and (c) specific coping strategies." (American Psychological Association, 2018)

Four specific approaches to counselling interventions have emerged that seem to be particularly helpful in helping individuals develop resilience with respect to stigma.

Supporting stigma resistance and building a stigma resistance ability.

In addition to coping skills training, some individuals may need help to learn how to differentiate their own thoughts and sense of self (and self-worth) from the thoughts of others before they can engage in directly confronting or challenging stigma (Firmin et al., 2017). They may also need professional help in developing self-compassion and self-validation.

Cognitive behaviour retraining with a focus on maladaptive responses, representation of self, and stigma coping strategies.

Supporting efforts to challenge self-stigma. Stereotype agreement is strongly correlated with self-concurrence and self-esteem decrement, as well as poor self-efficacy, and depression (Corrigan et al., 2006). These can all be the focus of either individual or group counselling.

Group work and peer-to-peer support and mentoring. Research suggests that being around similarly stigmatized others might reduce identity threat concerns. For example, people with stigmatized identities who encounter more people with similar stigmas report greater self-esteem (Frable, Platt & Hoey, 1998). Additionally, identity-based rejection sensitivity and distress may emerge from diminished access to similarly stigmatized others as identity group members (Cortopassi, Quinn & Nicolas, 2024).

8

Conclusion

We saw how helping people cope with stigma may improve their mental health and quality of life and help them participate in social, educational, and employment opportunities. We have also seen how stigma sometimes prevents individuals from seeking help for their problems or adhering to treatment. Supporting them as they struggle to cope with various and often intersecting stigmas will lead to better outcomes in healthcare and mental health and hopefully empower them to successfully manage difficult life transitions.

Within our own organization, we can encourage open and honest conversations about stigma and its impacts. We can learn to challenge our own biases and those that are reflected in our policies and practices. We can challenge stigmatization and discrimination whenever we encounter them. We can also strive to create safe spaces where individuals can discuss their experiences without fear of judgment. Implementing such strategies can significantly reduce stigma and create a more compassionate and inclusive environment. Everyone in the helping professions is encouraged to listen openly, patiently and attentively to what their clients dare to share with them about their experience of stigma.

Supporting someone affected by stigma involves a combination of empathy, understanding, and practical assistance. We tried to outline the main parameters of a stigma-informed practice, but we recognize that the effectiveness of stigma reduction and remediation strategies will vary greatly based on the context of the interventions and the target populations. There is much left to be learned about a stigma-informed practice and how it can be perfected and implemented.

We are grateful to the people who agreed to share their stories with us. These stories will hopefully help us build empathy and understanding and encourage open and honest conversations about stigma.

A commitment to an evidence-based approach dictated that we indulge in lengthy presentations of some of the voluminous research that exists on stigma. We hope that the readers were not too distracted by that and that they found multiple opportunities, as they were reading these pages, to reflect on their own experience of empowering people and helping them find healthy and self-affirming ways to cope with stigma.

References

Adams, E. B., Chen, E. Y., & Chapman, R. (2017). Erasing the mark of a criminal past: Ex-offenders' expectations and experiences with record clearance. *Punishment & Society*, 19(1), 23–52. https://doi.org/10.1177/1462474516645688

Addis, M. E., & Mahalik, J. R. (2003). Men, masculinity, and the contexts of help seeking. *American Psychologist*, 58(1), 5–14. https://doi.org/10.1037/0003-066x.58.1.5

Agan, A. & Starr, S. (2018) Ban the box, criminal records, and racial discrimination: A field experiment. *The Quarterly Journal of Economics*, 133(1), 191–235. https://doi.org/10.1093/qje/qjx028

Agterberg, S. (2018). Examining gendered treatment barriers among people with substance use and co-occurring mental health problems (Master of Arts Thesis, Carleton University).

Ali, A., Lyons, B., & Ryan, A. M. (2017). Managing a perilous stigma: Ex-offenders' use of reparative impression management tactics in hiring contexts. *Journal of Applied Psychology*, 102(9), 1271–1285. https://doi.org/10.1037/apl0000226

Allen, J, Copello, A, & Orford, J (2005). Fear during alcohol detoxification. *Journal of Health Psychology*, 10(4), 503–510. https://doi.org/10.1177/1359105305053414

Ameri, M., Kurtzberg, T.R. (2022). The disclosure dilemma: requesting accommodations for chronic pain in job interviews. *Journal of Cancer Survivorship*, 16(1), 152–164. https://doi.org/10.1007/s11764-021-01142-3

American Psychological Association (2018). *APA dictionary of psychology.* https://dictionary.apa.org/

Angermeyer, M. C. & Schomerus, G. (2017). State of the art of population-based attitude research on mental health: A systematic review. *Epidemiology and Psychiatric Science*, 26(3), 252-264. https://doi.org/10.1017/S2045796016000627.

Appelqvist-Schmidlechner, K., Haavalammi, N., & Kekonen, M. (2023). Benefits and underlying mechanisms of organized sport participation on mental health among socially vulnerable boys. *Sports and Society*, 26 (2), 240-262. https://doi.org/10.1080/17430437.2021.1996348

Armstrong, L. & Fraser, C. (2020). The disclosure dilemma: Stigma and talking about sex work in the decriminalised context. In: Armstrong, L., Abel, G. (Eds.) *Sex work and the New Zealand model: Decriminalisation and social change.* Bristol University Press, 177-198.

REFERENCES

Asiedu G, Myers-Bowman, K. (2014). Gender differences in the experiences of HIV/AIDS-related stigma: A qualitative study in Ghana. *Health Care Women International*, 35(7–9), 703–727. https://doi.org/10.1080/07399332.2014.895367

Ataro Z., Mengesha M. M., Abrham, A., & Digaffe, T. (2020). Gender differences in perceived stigma and coping strategies among people living with HIV/AIDS at Jugal Hospital, Harar, Ethiopia. *Psychology Research and Behavior Management*, 14(13), 1191–120. https://doi.org/10.2147/PRBM.S283969

Babchischin, K., Keown, L., & Mularczyk, K. (2021). Economic Outcomes of Canadian Federal Offenders. Ottawa: Public Safety Canada. https://www.public-safety.gc.ca/cnt/rsrcs/pblctns/2021-r002/2021-r002-en.pdf

Bachman, R., Rodriguez, S., Kerrison, E. M., & Leon, C. (2019). The recursive relationship between substance abuse, prostitution, and incarceration: Voices from a long-term cohort of women. *Victims & Offenders*, 14(5), 587-605. https://doi.org/10.1080/15564886.2019.1628146

Baert, S., De Visschere, S., Schoors, K., Vandenberghe, D., & Omey, E. (2016). First depressed, then discriminated against? *Social Science & Medicine*, 170, 247–254. https://doi.org/10.1016/j.socscimed.2016.06.033

Baffour, F. D., Francis, A., Chong, M., & Harris, N. (2023). Criminal records and post-prison employment in Ghana: Formal and informal means of performing criminal background checks. *Criminology & Criminal Justice*, 23(4), 629-647. https://doi.org/10.1177/17488958231161429

Barr, Û. & Rutter, N. (2022). Desistance and the stigma machine: Being a 'good woman'. In L. Baldwin (Ed.), *Gendered Justice*. Taylor and Francis.

Barr, Û. (2023). Working together? Gendered barriers to employment and desistance from harm amongst criminalised English women. *Feminist Criminology*, 18(2), 156–177. https://doi.org/10.1177/15570851231151728

Batastini, A. B., Bolaños, A. D., Morgan, R. D., & Mitchell, S. M. (2017). Bias in hiring applicants with mental illness and criminal justice involvement: A follow-up study with employers. *Criminal Justice and Behavior*, 44(6), 777–795. https://doi.org/10.1177/0093854817693663

Batchelder, A. W., Foley, J. D., Wirtz, M. R., Mayer, K., & O'Cleirigh, C. (2021). Substance use stigma, avoidance coping, and missed HIV appointments among MSM who use substances. *AIDS & Behavior*, 25(5), 1454–1463. https://doi.org/10.1007/s10461-020-02982-3

Baxter, A., Salmon, C., Dufresne, K., Carasco-Lee, A., & Matheson, F. I. (2016). Gender differences in felt stigma and barriers to help-seeking for problem gambling. *Addictive Behaviors Reports*, 3(3), 1–8. https://doi.org/10.1016/j.abrep.2015.10.001

Begum, T., Murrell, K., & Robinson-Barella, A. (2024). Tackling inequalities in access to medicines for people experiencing homelessness: A meta-ethnography and qualitative systematic review. *Health Expectations*, 27(5), e70076. https://doi.org//10.1111/hex.70076

Benoit, C, Jansson, M, Smith, M, & Flagg, J. (2018). Prostitution stigma and its effect on the working conditions, personal lives and health of sex workers. *Journal of Sex Research*, 55(4–5), 457–471. DOI: 10.1080/00224499.2017.1393652

Benoit, C, Smith, M, Jansson, M, Magnus, S., Maurice, R., Flagg, J., & Reist, D. (2019). Canadian sex workers weigh the costs and benefits of disclosing their occupational status to health providers. *Sexuality Research and Social Policy*, 16(3), 329–341. https://doi.org/10.1007/s13178-018-0339-8

Benoit, C., Maurice, R. Abel, G., Smith, M., Jansson, M., Healey, P., & Magnuson, D. (2020). 'I dodged the stigma bullet': Canadian sex workers' situated responses to occupational stigma. *Culture, Health & Sexuality*, 22(1), 81–95. https://doi.org/10.1080/13691058.2019.1576226

Benoit, C., McCarthy, B., & Jansson, M. (2015). Occupational stigma and mental health: Discrimination and depression among front-line service workers. *Canadian Public Policy*, 41(Supplement 2), S61-S69. https://doi.org/10.3138/cpp.2014-077

Benoit, C., McCarthy, B., & Jansson, M. (2015a). Stigma, sex work, and substance use: A comparative analysis. *Sociology of Health & Illness*, 37(3), 437–451. DOI: 10.1111/1467-9566.12201

Benoit, C., Ouellet, N., & Jansson, M. (2016). Unmet health care needs among sex workers in five census metropolitan areas of Canada. *Canadian Journal of Public Health*, 107(3), e266–e271. https://doi.org/10.17269/cjph.107.5178

Benoit, C., Smith, M., Jansson, M., Magnus, S., Flagg, J., & Maurice, R. (2018a). Sex work and three dimensions of self-esteem: Self-worth, authenticity and self-efficacy. *Culture, Health and Sexuality*, 20(1), 69-83. https://doi.org/10.1080/13691058.2017.1328075

Berry, M., & Wiener, R. (2020). Ex-offender housing stigma and discrimination. *Psychology, Public Policy, and Law*, 26(2), 213–232. https://doi.org/10.1037/law0000225.supp

Blakey, J. M. & Gunn, A. (2018). The "ickiness factor": Stigma as a barrier to exiting prostitution. *Journal of Offender Rehabilitation*, 57(8), 538-561. https://doi.org/10.1080/10509674.2018.1549177

Blitsa, D., Gouldin, L. P., Jacobs, J. B., & Larauri, E. (2015). Criminal records and immigration: Comparing the United States and the European Union. *Fordham International Law Journal* 39(2), 205–244.

Bloom, N., Guvenen, F., Smith, B. S., Song, J., & von Wachter, T. (2018). The disappearing large-firm wage premium. *AEA Papers and Proceedings*, 108 (May), 317–322.

Booth, N., Masson, I., & Baldwin, L. (2018). Promises, promises: Can the Female Offender Strategy deliver? *Probation Journal*, 65(4), 429-438. https://doi.org/10.1177/0264550518808363

Bos, A. et al. (2013). Stigma: Advances in theory and research. *Basic and Applied Social Psychology*, 35 (1), 1-9, https://doi.org/10.1080/01973533.2012.746147

Bossy, D., Knutsen, I.R., Rogers, A., & Foss, C. (2017). Group affiliation in self-management: support or threat to identity? *Health Expectations*, 20(1), 159-170. https://doi.org/10.1111/hex.12448

Bowen, R. & Bungay, V. (2016) Taint: an examination of the lived experiences of stigma and its lingering effects for eight sex industry experts. *Culture, Health and Sexuality*, 18(2),186-99. https://doi: 10.1080/13691058.2015.1072875.

Boyd, J. E., Adler, E., P., Otilingam, P. G. & Peters, T. (2014). Internalized stigma of mental illness (ISMI) scale: A multinational review. *Comprehensive Psychiatry*, 55(1), 221-231, https://doi.org/10.1016/j.comppsych.2013.06.005

Boyd, J. E., Hayward, H., Bassett, E. D., & Hoff, R. (2016). Internalized stigma of mental illness and depressive and psychotic symptoms in homeless veterans over 6 months. *Psychiatry Research*, 240, 253–259. https://doi.org/10.1016/j.psychres.2016.04.035

Braithwaite, J. (1989). *Crime, shame and reintegration*. Cambridge University Press.

Braithwaite, J. (1996). Restorative justice and a better future. *The Dalhousie Review*, 76(1), 9-31. https://dalspace.library.dal.ca/

Branigan, A. R., Ellis, R., Jacobsen, W. C., & Haskins, A. R. (2023). System management and compensatory parenting: Educational involvement after maternal incarceration. *Criminology*, 61, 482–517. https://doi.org/10.1111/1745-9125.12339

Brenner, R. E., Engel, K. E., Vogel, D. L., Tucker, J. R., Yamawaki, N., & Lannin, D. G. (2018). Intersecting cultural identities and help-seeking attitudes: the role of religious commitment, gender, and self-stigma of seeking help. *Mental Health, Religion & Culture*, 21(6), 578–587. https://doi.org/10.1080/13674676.2018.1519782

Brito, T. L., & Wood, K. (2023). Litigating precarity: Low-wage workers and child-support enforcement. *North Carolina Law Review*, 101(5), 1495–1548.

Brouwers, E. P. M. (2020). Social stigma is an underestimated contributing factor to unemployment in people with mental illness or mental health issues: Position paper and future directions. *BMC Psychology*, 8, 1–7. https://doi.org/10.1186/s40359-020-00399-0

Burgess, A., Bauer, E., Gallagher, S., Karstens, B., Lavoie, L., Ahrens, K., O'Connor, A. (2021). Experiences of stigma among individuals in recovery from opioid use disorder in a rural setting: A qualitative analysis. *Journal of Substance Abuse Treatment*, 130, 108488. https:// doi.org/10.1016/j.jsat.2021.108488

Butler, L., Cullen, C., Burton, F. T., Velmer S. (2023). Racial attitudes and belief in redeemability: Most Whites believe justice-involved Black people can change. *Criminology*. 61(2), 316–353. https://doi.org/10.1111/1745-9125.12331

Canham, S. L., Weldrick, R., Erisman, M., McNamara, A, Rose, J. N., Siantz, E., Casucci, T., & McFarland, M. M. (2024). A scoping review of the experiences and outcomes of stigma and discrimination towards persons experiencing homelessness,

Health & Social Care in the Community, 2060619. https://doi.org/10.1155/2024/2060619

Cardona, N. D., Cohen, J. M., & Feinstein, B. A. (2023). Targeting Self-Compassion Among Sexual and Gender Minority People Experiencing Psychological Distress. *Clinical Psychology: Science and Practice*, 30(1), 40–42. https://doi.org/10.1037/cps0000116

Carlson, C. E., Witte, S. S., Pala, A. N., Tsai, L. C., Wainberg, M., & Aira, T. (2017). The impact of violence, perceived stigma, and other work-related stressors on depressive symptoms among women engaged in sex work. *Global Social Welfare*, 4(2), 51–57. https://doi.org/10.1007/s40609-017-0085-5.

Carlton, B. & Segrave, M. (2011). Women's survival post-imprisonment: Connecting imprisonment with pains past and present. *Punishment and Society*, 13(5), 551-570. https://doi.org/10.1177/1462474511422174

Carrara, B. S., & Ventura, C. A. A. (2018). Self-stigma, mentally ill persons and health services: An integrative review of literature. *Archives of Psychiatric Nursing*, 32(2), 317–324. https://doi.org/10.1016/j.apnu.2017.11.001

Carrara, B. S., Bobbili, S. J., & Ventura, C. A. A. (2023). Community Health Workers and Stigma Associated with Mental Illness: An Integrative Literature Review. *Community Mental Health Journal*, 59(1), 132–159. https://doi.org/10.1007/s10597-022-00993-z

Case, S. (2007). Questioning the 'evidence' of risk that underpins evidence-led youth justice interventions, *Youth Justice*, 7(2), 91–105. https://doi.org/10.1177/147322540707877

Case, S. and Haines, K. (2010). Risky business? The risk in risk factor research. *Criminal Justice Matters*, 80(1), 20–22. https://doi.org/10.1080/09627251.2010.482234

Castle, A. (2023). *Considering the best interests of the child in sentencing and other decisions concerning parents facing criminal sanctions: An overview for practitioners.* Vancouver: ICCLR & EFry.

Celeste-Villalvir, A., Payan, D. D., Armenta, G., Palar, K., Then-Paulino, A., Acevedo, R., Fulcar, M. A., & Derose, K. P. (2023). Exploring gender differences in HIV-related stigma and social support in a low-resource setting: A qualitative study in the Dominican Republic. *PLoS ONE*, 18(8), 1–22. https://doi.org/10.1371/journal.pone.0290228

Celinska, K. (2000). Volunteer involvement in ex-offenders' readjustment: Reducing the stigma of imprisonment. *Journal of Offender Rehabilitation*, 30(3–4), 99–116. https://doi.org/10.1300/J076v30n03_05

Cerda-Jara, M. & Harding. D. J. (2024). Criminal record stigma in the labor market for college graduates: A mixed methods study. *Sociological Science*, 11, 41–66. https://doi.org/10.15195/v11.a2

Cerda-Jara, M., Elster, A., & Harding, D. J. (2020). Criminal record stigma in the college-educated labor market. Institute for Research on Labor and Employment. https://irle. berkeley. edu/files/2020/05/Harding _ Jara-Cerda-Elster-brief. pdf

Chamberlain, J. M. (2013). Sports-based intervention and the problem of youth offending: A diverse enough tool for a diverse society? *Sport in Society*, 16(10), 1279–1292. https://doi.org/10.1080/17430437.2013.821251

Chan, K. K. S., Fung, W. T. W., Leung, D. C. K., & Tsui, J. K. C. (2022). The impact of perceived and internalised stigma on clinical and functional recovery among people with mental illness. *Health & Social Care in the Community*, 30(6), e6102–e6111. https://doi.org/10.1111/hsc.14047

Chaudoir, S. R. & Quinn, D. M. (2010). Disclosing concealable stigmatized identities: The impact of disclosure motivations and positive first disclosure experiences on fear of disclosure and well-being. *Journal of Social Issues*, 66(3), 570–584. https://doi.org/10.1111/j.1540-4560.2010.01663.x

Chin, V. & Dandurand, Y. (2018). *Introductory handbook on the prevention of recidivism and the social reintegration of offenders*. Vienna: United Nations on Drug and Crime. https://www.unodc.org/documents/justice-and-prison-reform/18-02303_ebook.pdf

Cihangir, S., Barreto, M., & Ellemers, N. (2011). The dark side of ambiguous discrimination: How state self-esteem moderates emotional and behavioural responses to ambiguous and unambiguous discrimination. *British Journal of Social Psychology*, 49(1), 155–174. https://doi.org/10.1348/014466609X425869

Cipollina, R., Sanchez, D. T., & Mikrut, E. E. (2024). Disclosing mental illness to share or test stigma? Disclosure motivations and disclosure directness. *Stigma and Health*. 9(3), 268–277. https://doi.org/10.1037/sah0000428

Cleary, A. (2017). Help-seeking patterns and attitudes to treatment amongst men who attempted suicide. *Journal of Mental Health*, 26(3), 220–224. https://doi:10.3109/09638237.2016.1149800

Coker, A. L., Smith, P. H., Thompson, M. P., McKeown, R. E., Bethea, L., & Davis, K. E. (2002). Social support protects against the negative effects of partner violence on mental health. *Journal of Women's Health & Gender-Based Medicine*, 11(5), 465–476.

Colombini, M., Mutemwa, R., Kivunaga, J., Moore, L. S., & Mayhew, S. H. (2014). Experiences of stigma among women living with HIV attending sexual and reproductive health services in Kenya: A qualitative study. *BMC Health Services Research*, 14, 412. http://www.biomedcentral.com/1472-6963/14/412

Conklin, T. M. (2021). Mental illness stigma: Strategies to address a barrier to care. Women's Healthcare: *A Clinical Journal for NPs*, 9(2), 16–20. https://doi.org/10.51256/whc042116

Cook, H., Husein, S., Ahmadi, R., Tasca, J., & Abbot-Mcleod, A. (2024). Not in my workplace: Addressing workplace exclusion of individuals with criminal records.

John Howard Society of Ontario. https://johnhoward.on.ca/wp-content/uploads/2024/01/Not-in-My-Workplace-Report-Final.pdf

Corda, A. & Lageson, S. (2020) Disordered punishment: Workaround technologies of criminal records disclosure and the rise of a new penal entrepreneurialism. *British Journal of Criminology* 60(2), 245–264. https://doi.org/10.1093/bjc/azz039

Corda, A. (2016) More justice and less harm: Reinventing access to criminal history records. *Howard Law Journal* 60(1), 1–60. https://ssrn.com/abstract=2822386

Corrigan, P. W., & Rao, D. (2012). On the self-stigma of mental illness: Stages, disclosure, and strategies for change. *Canadian Journal of Psychiatry*, 57(8), 464–469. https://doi.org/10.1177/070674371205700804

Corrigan, P. W., Kosyluk, K. A., & Rüsch, N. (2013). Reducing self-stigma by coming out proud. *American Journal of Public Health*, 103(5), 794–800. https://doi.org/10.2105/AJPH.2012.301037

Corrigan, P. W., Lara, J. L., Shah, B. B., Mitchell, K. T., Simmes, D., & Jones, K. L. (2017). The public stigma of birth mothers of children with fetal alcohol spectrum. *Alcohol: Clinical and Experimental Research*, 41(6), 1166–1173. https://doi.org/10.1111/acer.13381.

Corrigan, P. W., Morris, S., Larson, J., Rafacz, J., Wassel, A., Michaels, P., Wilkniss, S., Batia, K., & Rüsch, N. (2010). Self stigma and coming out about one's mental illness. *Journal of Community Psychology*, 38(3), 259–275. https://doi,org/10.1002/jcop.20363

Corrigan, P. W., Nieweglowski, K., & Sayer, J. (2019). Self-stigma and the mediating impact of the "why try" effect on depression. *Journal of Community Psychology*, 47(3), 698–705. https://doi.org/10.1002/jcop.22144

Corrigan, P. W., Watson, A. C., & Barr, L. (2006). The self–stigma of mental illness: Implications for self–esteem and self–efficacy. *Journal of Social and Clinical Psychology*, 25(8), 875–884. https://doi.org/10.1521/jscp.2006.25.8.875

Corrigan, P., Larson, J., & Rusch N. (2009). Self-stigma and the "why try" effect: Impact on life goals and evidence-based practices. *World Psychiatry*. 8:75–81. https://doi.org/10.1002/j.2051-5545.2009.tb00218.x

Cortopassi, A. C., Quinn, D. M., & Nicolas, G. (2024). The identity group as a source of social influence for individuals with concealable stigmatized identities. *PLoS One*, 19(9), e0309687. https://doi.org/10.1371/journal.pone.0309687.

Crapanzano, K. A., Hammarlund, R., Ahmad, B., Hunsinger, N., & Kullar, R. (2018). The association between perceived stigma and substance use disorder treatment outcomes: a review. *Substance Abuse and Rehabilitation*, 27(10), 1-12. https://doi.org/10.2147/SAR.S183252.

Cremin, K., Healy, O., Spirtos, M., & Quinn, S. (2021). Autism awareness interventions for children and adolescents: A scoping review. *Journal of Developmental and Physical Disabilities*, 33(1), 27-50. https://doi.org/10.1007/s10882-020-09741-1

Cumming, C., Troeung, L., Young, J. T., Kelty, E., & Preen, D. B. (2016). Barriers to accessing methamphetamine treatment: A systematic review and meta-analysis. *Drug and Alcohol Dependence*, 168, 263–273. https://doi.org/10.1016/j.drugalcdep.2016.10.001

Cunningham, J. A., Sobell, L. C., Sobell, M. B., Agrawal, S., & Toneatto, T. (1993). Barriers to treatment: why alcohol and drug abusers delay or never seek treatment. *Addictive Behaviors*, 18(3), 347–353. Retrieved from http://www.ncbi.nlm.nih.gov/pubmed/8393611

Dąbrowska, K. & Wieczorek, T. (2020). Perceived social stigmatisation of gambling disorders and coping with stigma. Nordic Studies on Alcohol and Drugs, 37(3), 279-297. https:/doi.org/10.1177/1455072520902342

Dandurand, Y. & Heidt, J (2023). *Youth crime prevention and sports*. Bristol: Bristol University Press.

Davern, J., O'Donnell, A. T., & Picardo, M. (2018). Stigma predicts health-related quality of life impairment, psychological distress, and somatic symptoms in acne sufferers. *PLoS One*, 13(9), e0205009. https://doi.org/10.1371/journal.pone.0205009

Davis, L. & Shlafer, R. J. (2017). Mental health of adolescents with currently and formerly incarcerated parents. *Journal of Adolescence*, 54, 120–134. https://doi.org/10.1016/j.adolescence.2016.10.006

Day, A.-M. (2022). 'It's a hard balance to find': The perspectives of youth justice practitioners in England on the place of 'risk' in an emerging 'child-first' world. *Youth Justice*, 23(1), 58-75. https://doi.org/10.1177/14732254221075205

De Boeck, A., Pleysier, S., & Put, J. (2018). The social origins of gender differences in anticipated feelings of guilt and shame following delinquency. *Criminology & Criminal Justice* 18(3), 291–313. https://doi.org/10.1177/1748895817721273

Deakin, J., Fox, C., & Matos, R. (2022). Labelled as 'risky' in an era of control: How young people experience and respond to the stigma of criminalized identities. *European Journal of Criminology*, 19(4), 653–673. https://doi.org/10.1177/1477370820916728

Decker, G. (2021). Occupational licensing as a barrier for people with criminal records: Proposals to improve anti-discrimination law to address adverse employment impacts from the criminal legal system. *Fordham Urban Law Journal*, 49(1), 189–219.

DeMarco, L. M. (2023). Criminal record stigma, race, and neighborhood inequality. *Criminology: An Interdisciplinary Journal*. 61(4), 705–730. https://doi.org/10.1111/1745-9125.12347

Denver, M., & Ewald, A. (2018). Credentialing decisions and criminal records: A narrative approach. *Criminology*, 56(4), 715–749. https://doi.org/10.1111/1745-9125.12190

Dhillon, J., Horch, J. D., & Hodgins, D. C. (2011). Cultural influences on stigmatization of problem gambling: East Asian and Caucasian Canadians. *Journal of Gambling Studies*, 27(4), 633–647. https://doi.org/10.1007/s10899-010-9233-x

Durnescu, I. (2021). Work as a drama: The experience of former prisoners in the labour market, *European Journal of Criminology,* 18(2), 170-191. https://doi.org/10.1177/1477370819838718

Durso, L. E, Latner, J. D., & Ciao, A. C. (2016). Weight bias internalization in treatment-seeking overweight adults: Psychometric validation and associations with self-esteem, body image, and mood symptoms. *Eating Behavior,* (21)1, 104–108. https://doi.org/10.1016/j.eatbeh.2016.01.011

Eckholm, D. (2019). Sport as a means of governing social integration: Discourses on bridging and bonding social relations. *Sociology of Sport Journal,* 36(2): 152–161. https://doi.org/10.1123/ssj.2018-0099

Eckstein, J. J. (2015). IPV Stigma and its social management: The roles of relationship-type, abuse-type, and victims' sex. *Journal of Family Violence,* 31(2), 1–11. doi:10.1007/s10896-015-9752-4.

EFry (2019). *Supporting children with incarcerated parents: A community guide.* Vancouver: Elizabeth Fry Society of Greater Vancouver.

Ellis, R. (2020). Redemption and reproach: Religion and carceral control in action among women in prison, *Criminology,* 58(4), 747--772. 26p. DOI: 10.1111/1745-9125.12258.

Engel, C. S., & Sheppard, E. (2020). Can cartoons which depict autistic characters improve attitudes towards autistic peers? *Journal of Autism and Developmental Disorders,* 50(3), 1007–1017. https://doi.org/10.1007/s10803-019-04318-0

Estrada F. & Nilsson A. (2012). Does it cost more to be a female offender? A life-course study of childhood circumstances, crime, drug abuse, and living conditions. *Feminist Criminology* 7(3), 196–219. https://doi.org/10.1177/15570851114297

Evans, D. N. (2016). The effect of criminal convictions on real estate agent decisions in New York City. *Journal of Crime & Justice,* 39(3), 363–379. https://doi.org/10.1080/0735648X.2016.1166068

Evans, D. N. (2019). Full disclosure: experimental analysis of female online dating on parole. *Journal of Experimental Criminology,* 15(2), 179–199. https://doi.org/10.1007/s11292-019-09357-2

Evans, D. N., & Blount-Hill, K. L. (2022). Swipe right? Experimental Analyses of App-Based Dating in the Age of Criminal Stigma. *Corrections,* 7(4), 296–318. https://doi.org/10.1080/23774657.2020.1799726

Evans, D. N., Blount-Hill, K.-L., & Cubellis, M. A. (2019). Examining housing discrimination across race, gender and felony history. Housing Studies, 34(5), 761–778. https://doi.org/10.1080/02673037.2018.1478069

Evans, D., & Porter, J. (2015). Criminal history and landlord rental decisions: a New York quasi-experimental study. Journal of Experimental Criminology, 11(1), 21–42. https://doi.org/10.1007/s11292-014-9217-4

Evans, N. A, (2022). Coping with gendered welfare stigma: Exploring everyday accounts of stigma and resistance strategies among mother who claim social security benefits. *Social Policy and Society*, 21(4), 690–700. https://doi.org/10.1017/S1474746422000070

Fang, M., Li, G., Kang, X., Hou, F., Lv, G., Xu, X., Kong, L., & Li, P. (2021). The role of gender and self-esteem as moderators of the relationship between stigma and psychological distress among infertile couples. *Psychology, Health & Medicine*, 26(10), 1181–1194. https://doi.org/10.1080/13548506.2020.1808233

Farmer (Lord) (2019). *The importance of strengthening female offenders' family and other relationships to prevent reoffending and reduce intergenerational crime*. Final report from the Lord Farmer review for women: Ministry of Justice (UK).

Farrall, S. (2019). *The architecture of desistance*. Abingdon: Routledge.

Farrugia, A., Pienaar, K., Fraser, S., Edwards, M., & Madden, A. (2021). Basic care as exceptional care: Addiction stigma and consumer accounts of quality healthcare in Australia. *Health Sociology Review*, 30(2), 95–110. https://doi.org/10.1080/14461242.2020.1789485

Finlay, K., Mueller-Smith, M., & Street, B. (2023). Criminal justice involvement, self-employment, and barriers in recent public policy. *Journal of Policy Analysis and Management*, 42(1), 11–34. https://doi.org/10.1002/pam.22438

Firmin, R. L., Luther, L., Lysaker, P. H., Minor, K. S., & Salyers, M. P. (2016). Stigma resistance is positively associated with psychiatric and psychosocial outcomes: A meta-analysis. *Schizophrenia Research*, 175(1–3), 118–128. https://doi.org/10.1016/j.schres.2016.03.008

Firmin, R. L., Luther, L., Lysaker, P. H., Minor, K. S., McGrew, J. H., Cornwell, M. N., & Salyers, M. P. (2017). Stigma resistance at the personal, peer, and public levels: A new conceptual model. *Stigma and Health*, 2(3), 182–194. https://doi.org/10.1037/sah0000054

Firmin, R. L., Lysaker, P. H., Luther, L., Yanos, P. T., Leonhardt, B., Breier, A., & Vohs, J. L. (2019). Internalized stigma in adults with early phase versus prolonged psychosis. *Early Intervention in Psychiatry*, 13(4), 745–751. https://doi.org/10.1111/eip.12553

Firmin, R. L., Lysaker, P. H., McGrew, J. H., Minor, K. S., Luther, L., & Salyers, M. P. (2017a). The Stigma Resistance Scale: A multi-sample validation of a new instrument to assess mental illness stigma resistance. *Psychiatry Research*, 258, 37–43. https://doi.org/10.1016/j.psychres.2017.09.063

Ford, R., 2011. Interpersonal challenges as a constraint on care: the experience of nurses' care of patients who use illicit drugs. *Contemporary Nursing*, 37(2), 241–252. https://doi.org/10.5172/conu.2011.37.2.241

Foster, S. & Doksum, T. (2019). Community-driven strategies to address stigma and build healthier communities in Maine. *Maine Health Access Foundation*. https://mehaf.org/wp-content/uploads/Community-Driven-Strategies-to-Address-Stigma-and-Build-Healthier-Communities-in-Maine.pdf

Fox, A. B., & Earnshaw, V. A. (2023). The relationship between mental illness stigma and self-labeling. *Psychiatric Rehabilitation Journal*, 46(2), 127–136. https://doi.org/10.1037/prj0000552

Fox, A. B., Smith, B. N., & Vogt, D. (2016). The relationship between anticipated stigma and work functioning for individuals with depression. *Journal of Social and Clinical Psychology*, 35(10), 883–897. https://doi.org/10.1521/jscp.2016.35.10.883

Fox, A. B., Smith, B. N., & Vogt, D. (2018). How and when does mental illness stigma impact treatment seeking? Longitudinal examination of relationships between anticipated and internalized stigma, symptom severity, and mental health service use. *Psychiatry Research*, 268, 15–20. https://doi.org/10.1016/j.psychres.2018.06.036

Frable, D. E., Platt, L., & Hoey, S. (1998). Concealable stigmas and positive self-perceptions: feeling better around similar others. *Journal of Personality and Social Psychology*, 74(4), 909-22. https://doi.org/10.1037//0022-3514.74.4.909

Fredrikson, T. and Gålnander, R. (2020). Fearful futures and haunting histories in women's desistance from crime: A longitudinal study of desistance as an uncanny process. *Criminology*, 58(4), 599-618. https://doi.org/10.1111/1745-9125.12250

Furst, R. T., & Evans, D. N. (2017). Renting apartments to felons: Variations in real estate agent decisions due to stigma. *Deviant Behavior*, 38(6), 698–708. https://doi.org/10.1080/01639625.2016.1197635

Gålnander, R. (2020). "Shark in the fish tank": Secrets and stigma in relational desistance from crime. *British Journal of Criminology*, 60(5), 1302–1319. https://doi.org/10.1093/bjc/azaa015

Gardner, D. M., Ali, A. A., & Ryan, A. M. (2023). Reparative impression management for ex-offender applicants: Understanding mechanisms, race/ethnicity, and disclosure timing. *Journal of Business and Psychology*, 38(3), 561–587. https://doi.org/10.1007/s10869-023-09880-0

Garside, R. (2009). Risky individuals, risky families or risky societies? *Criminal Justice Matters*, 78(1), 42–43. https://doi.org/10.1080/09627250903385305

Gerrish, S. E. (2021). Diagnosis disclosure: The impact of gender and stigma. *Modern Psychological Studies*, 26(2), Article 1.

Glanton, C., Cucciare, M., & Epstein, E. E. (2020). Sex and gender effects in recovery from alcohol use disorder. *Alcohol Research: Current Reviews*, 40(3), 1–19. https://doi.org/10.35946/arcr.v40.3.03

Goffman, E. (1959). *The presentation of self in everyday life*. New York: Anchor Books

Goffman, E. (1963). *Stigma: Notes on the management of spoiled identity*. New York: Simon & Schuster.

Goffman, E. (1967). *Interaction ritual: Essays on face-to-face behavior*. New York: Pantheon Books.

Gonzales, L., Davidoff, K. C., Nadal, K. L., & Yanos, P. T. (2015). Microaggressions experienced by persons with mental illnesses: An exploratory study. *Psychiatric Rehabilitation Journal*, 38(3), 234–241. https://doi.org/10.1037/prj0000096

Grace, A. (2022). 'Get to know me, not the inmate': Women's management of the stigma of criminal records. *The British Journal of Criminology*, 62(1), 73–89. https://doi.org/10.1093/bjc/azab029

Griffin, N., Loucks, N., Minson, S., Shidrick, T., Young, T., Crowe, L., & Scott, S. (2025). *Divided households - Supporting children and young people with a family member in prison*. Newcastle University, Newcastle, UK. https://issuu.com/niftyfoxcreative/docs/newc_0342_divided_households_final_web

Hackler, A. H., Cornish, M. A., & Vogel, D. L. (2016). Reducing mental illness stigma: Effectiveness of hearing about the normative experiences of others. *Stigma and Health*, 1(3), 201–205. https://doi.org/10.1037/sah0000028

Ham, J., & Gilmour, F. (2017). 'We all have one': exit plans as a professional strategy in sex work. *Work, Employment and Society*, 31 (5), 748–763. https://doi.org/10.1177/0950017016666198

Hamilton, L. J., Coleman, M. E. & Krendl, A. C. (2023). Contact reduces substance use stigma through bad character attributions, especially for U.S. health care professionals. *Psychology of Addictive Behaviors*, 37(6), 734-745. https://doi.org/10.1037/adb0000953

Hammer, J. H., Vogel, D. L., & Heimerdinger-Edwards, S. R. (2013). Men's help seeking: Examination of differences across community size, education, and income. *Psychology of Men & Masculinity*, 14(1), 65–75. https://doi.org/10.1037/a0026813

Hamovitch, L., Pejic, S., Zannella, L., & Deska, J. C. (2023). Examining the effect of prison time on landlords' willingness to rent to exonerees: A test of the stigma-by-association framework. *Behavioral Sciences & the Law*, 41(2-3), 78–95. https://doi.org/10.1002/bsl.2608

Harding, D. J. (2003). Jean Valjean's dilemma: The management of ex-convict identity in the search for employment. *Deviant Behavior*, 24(6), 571–595. https://doi.org/10.1080/713840275

Harragan, A., Deakin, J., Fox, C., & Kaur, B. (2018). *"Risky youth" and criminalised identities*. Manchester: University of Manchester. https://www.promise.manchester.ac.uk/wp-content/uploads/2019/03/Individual-case-study-UK-Risky-youth.pdf

Hartog, K., Hubbard, C. D., Krouwer, A.F., Thornicroft, G., Kohrt, B. A., & Jordans, M. J. D. S. (2020). Stigma reduction interventions for children and adolescents in low- and middle-income countries: Systematic review of intervention strategies. *Social Science & Medicine*, 246, 112749. https://doi.org/10.1016/j.socscimed.2019.112749

Hatzenbuehler, M., Phelan, J., & Link, B. (2013). Stigma as a fundamental cause of population health inequalities. *American Journal of Public Health*, 103, 813–821. https://doi.org/10.2105/AJPH.2012.301069.

Hays, S. (1996). *The cultural contradictions of motherhood*. New Haven: Yale University Press.

Heath, P. J., Brenner, R. E., Vogel, D. L., Lannin, D. G., & Strass, H. A. (2017). Masculinity and barriers to seeking counseling: The buffering role of self-compassion. *Journal of Counseling Psychology*, 64(1), 94–103. https://doi.org/10.1037/cou0000185

Helminen, E. C., Ducar, D. M., Scheer, J. R., Parke, K. L., Morton, M. L., & Felver, J. C. (2023). Self-compassion, minority stress, and mental health in sexual and gender minority populations: A meta-analysis and systematic review. *Clinical Psychology: Science and Practice*, 30(1), 26-30. https://doi.org/10.1037/cps0000104

Hernandez Fernandes, R. H., Carrara, B. S., Andrade Vidigal, B. A., Barbosa Martins, A. L., Bobbili, S. J., & Arena Ventura, C. A. (2022). Stigma experienced by people with mental illness in South America: an integrative review. *Revista Cuidarte*, 13(2), 1–19. https://doi.org/10.15649/cuidarte.2014

Hicken, M. T., Lee, H., Ailshire, J., Burgard, S. A., & Williams, D. RE. (2013). "Every shut eye, ain't sleep": The role of racism-related vigilance in racial/ethnic disparities in sleep difficulty. Race and Social Problems, 5(1), 100–112. https://doi.org/10.1007/s12552-013-9095-9

Himmelstein, M. S., Puhl, R. M., & Quinn, D. M. (2017). Intersectionality: An understudied framework for addressing weight stigma. *American Journal of Preventive Medicine*, 53(4), 421–431. https://doi.org/10.1016/j.amepre.2017.04.003

Himmelstein, M. S., Young, D. M., Sanchez, D. T., & Jackson, J. S. (2015). Vigilance in the discrimination-stress model for Black Americans. *Psychological Health*, 30(3), 253–267. https://doi.org/10.1080/08870446.2014.966104.

Hing, N., Russell, A. M. T., & Gainsbury, S. M. (2016). Unpacking the public stigma of problem gambling: The process of stigma creation and predictors of social distancing. *Journal of Behavioral Addictions*, 5(3), 448–456. https://doi.org/10.1556/2006.5.2016.057

Hing, N. & Russell, A. M. T. (2017). Psychological factors, sociodemographic characteristics, and coping mechanisms associated with the self-stigma of problem gambling. *Journal of Behavioral Addictions*, 6(3), 416–424. https://doi.org/10.1556/2006.6.2017.056

Hing, N., Holdsworth, L., Tiyce, M., & Breen, H. (2013). Stigma and problem gambling: Current knowledge and future research directions. *International Gambling Studies*, 14(1), 64–81. https://doi.org/10.1080/14459795.2013.841722

Hing, N., Nuske, E., Gainsbury, S. M., & Russell, A. M. T. (2015). Perceived stigma and self-stigma of problem gambling: Perspectives of people with gambling problems. *International Gambling Studies*, 16(1), 31–48. https://doi.org/10.1080/14459795.2015.1092566.

Hipes, C., Lucas, J., Phelan, J. C., & White, R. C. (2016). The stigma of mental illness in the labor market. *Social Science Research*, 56, 16–25. https://doi.org/10.1016/j.ssresearch.2015.12.001

Howard, H. (2015). Reducing stigma: Lessons from opioid-dependent women. *Journal of Social Work Practice in the Addictions*, 15 (4), 418–438. https://doi.org/10.1080/1533256X.2015.1091003

Hunter, B. & Farrall, S. (2018). Emotions, future selves, and the process of desistance. *British Journal of Criminology*, 58(2), 291–308. https://doi.org/10.1093/bjc/azx017

Huskin, P. R., Reiser-Robbins, C., & Kwon, S. (2018). Attitudes of undergraduate students toward persons with disabilities: Exploring effects of contact experience on social distance across ten disability types. *Rehabilitation Counseling Bulletin*, 62(1), 53-63. https://doi.org/10.1177/003435521772760

Ispa-Landa, S. & Loeffler, C. (2016). Indefinite punishment and the criminal record: Stigma reports among expungement-seekers in Illinois. *Criminology*, 54, 387–412. https://doi.org/10.1111/1745-9125.12108

Ispa-Landa, S. (2019). Believing in a positive future as a form of stigma resistance: Narratives of denied expungement-seekers. *Deviant Behavior*, 40(11), 1428–1444. https://doi.org/10.1080/01639625.2019.1596550

Jackson, A. & Shannon, L. (2012). Barriers to receiving substance abuse treatment among rural pregnant women in Kentucky. *Maternal and Child Health Journal*, 16, 1762–1770. https://doi.org/10.1007/s10995-011-0923-5.

Johnstone, M., Jetten, J., Dingle, G. A., Parsell, C., & Walter, Z. C. (2015). Discrimination and well-being amongst the homeless: the role of multiple group membership. *Frontier in Psychology*, 1(6),739. https://doi.org/10.3389/fpsyg.2015.00739.

Jordan, U. (2022). "I feel like I'm useful. I'm not useless, you know?": Exploring Volunteering as Resistance to Stigma for Men Who Experience Mental Illness. *Social Policy & Society*, 11(4), 668–678. doi:10.1017/S1474746422000045

Judd, H., Yaugher, A. C., O'Shay, S., & Meier, C. L. (2023). Understanding stigma through the lived experiences of people with opioid use disorder. *Drug and Alcohol Dependence*, 249, 110873. https://doi.org/10.1016/j.drugalcdep.2023.110873

Kao, Y.-C., Lien, Y.-J., Chang, H.-A., Tzeng, N.-S., Yeh, C.-B., & Loh, C.-H. (2017). Stigma resistance in stable schizophrenia: The relative contributions of stereotype endorsement, self-reflection, self-esteem, and coping styles. *The Canadian Journal of Psychiatry*, 62(10), 735–744. https://doi.org/10.1177/0706743717730827

Karantzas, G. C., Younan, R., & Pilkington, P. D. (2023). The associations between early maladaptive schemas and adult attachment styles: A meta-analysis. *Clinical Psychology: Science and Practice*, 30(1), 1–20. https://doi.org/10.1037/cps0000108

Karantzas, G. C., Simpson, J. A., & Haslam, N. (2023). Dehumanization: Beyond the intergroup to the interpersonal. *Current Directions in Psychological Science*, 32(6), 501–507. https://doi.org/10.1177/09637214231204196

Keene, D. E., Smoyer, A. B., & Blankenship, K. M. (2018). Stigma, housing and identity after prison. *The Sociological Review*, 66(4), 799–815. https://doi.org/10.1177/0038026118777447

Kido, Y., Kawakami, N., Miyamoto, Y., Chiba, R., & Tsuchiya, M. (2013). Social capital and stigma toward people with mental illness in Tokyo, Japan. *Community Mental Health Journal*, 49(3), 243–247. https://doi.org/10.1007/s10597-012-9548-4

Kjellstrand, J. M. & Eddy, J. M. (2011). Parental Incarceration during Childhood, Family Context, and Youth Problem Behavior across Adolescence. *Journal of Offender Rehabilitation*, 50(1), 18–36. https://doi.org/10.1080/10509674.2011.536720

Koken, J. A. (2012). Independent female escort's strategies for coping with sex work related stigma. *Sexuality and Culture*, 16 (3), 209–229. https://doi.org/10.1007/s12119-011-9120-3

Konvisser, Z. D. (2015). What happened to me can happen to anybody: Women exonerees speak out. *Texas A&M Law Review*, 3(2). 303–366. https://doi.org/10.37419/LR.V3.I2.4.

Krüsi, A., Kerr, T., Taylor, C., Rhodes, T., & Shannon, K. (2016) 'They won't change it back in their heads that we're trash': the intersection of sex work-related stigma and evolving policing strategies. *Sociology of Health and Illness*, 38(7),1137–50. https://doi.org/10.1111/1467-9566.12436.

Kukucka, J., Applegarth, H. K., & Mello, A. L. (2020). Do exonerees face employment discrimination similar to actual offenders? *Legal and Criminological Psychology*, 25, 17–32. https://doi.org/10.1111/lcrp.12159

Kukucka, J., Clow, K., Horodyski, A., Deegan, K., & Gayleard, N. (2021). Do exonerees face housing discrimination? An email-based field experiment and content analysis. *Psychology, Public Policy, and Law*, 27(4), 570–580. https://doi.org/10.1037/law0000323

Lageson, S. E. (2016). Found Out and Opting Out: The Consequences of Online Criminal Records for Families. *Annals of the American Academy of Political and Social Science*, 665(1), 127–141. https://doi.org/10.1177/0002716215625053

Lageson, S. E. & Maruna, S. M. (2018). Digital degradation: Stigma management in the Internet age. *Punishment and Society*, 20(1), 113-133. https://doi.org/10.1177/1462474517737050

Lageson, S. E. (2016). Found Out and Opting Out: The Consequences of Online Criminal Records for Families. *Annals of the American Academy of Political and Social Science*, 665(1), 127–141. https://doi.org/10.1177/0002716215625053

Lageson, S. E. (2022). Criminal record stigma and surveillance in the digital age. *Annual Review of Criminology*, 5, 67–90. https://doi.org/10.1146/annurev-criminol-030920-092833

Lageson, S. E., Webster, E., & Sandoval, J. R. (2021). Digitizing and disclosing personal data: the proliferation of state criminal records on the internet. *Law & Social Inquiry*, 46(3), 635-665. doi:10.1017/lsi.2020.37

Lander, I. (2015). Gender, aging and drug use: A post-structural approach to the life course. *British Journal of Criminology*, 55(4), 270–85. http:// https://doi.org/10.1093/bjc/azu099

Lannin, D. G., Guyll, M., Vogel, D. L., & Madon, S. (2013). Reducing the stigma associated with seeking psychotherapy through self-affirmation. *Journal of Counseling Psychology*, 60(4), 508–519. http://dx.doi.org/10.1037/a0033789

Lannin, D. G., Vogel, D. L., Brenner, R. E., Abraham, W. T., & Heath, P. J. (2016). Does self-stigma reduce the probability of seeking mental health information? *Journal of Counseling Psychology*, 63(3), 351–358. http://dx.doi.org/10.1037/cou0000108

Lannin, D., Vogel, D. L., Brenner, R. E., & Tucker, J. (2015). Predicting distress and intentions to seek psychological help: The internalized stigma model. *The Counseling Psychologist*, 43, 64–93. https://doi.org/10.1177/0011000014541550

Latkin, C., Davey-Rothwell, M., Yang, J. Y., Crawford, N. (2013). The relationship between drug user stigma and depression among inner-city drug users in Baltimore, MD. *Journal of Urban Health*, 90(1), 147–156. 10.1007/s11524-012-9753-z

Lawrence, J. W., Fauerbach, J. A., Heinberg, L. J., Doctor, M., & Thombs, B. D. (2006). The reliability and validity of the Perceived Stigmatization Questionnaire (PSQ) and the Social Comfort Questionnaire (SCQ) among an adult burn survivor sample. *Psychological Assessment*, 18(1), 106–111. https://doi.org/10.1037/1040-3590.18.1.106

Leasure, P. & Stevens Andersen, T. (2016). Recognizing redemption: Old criminal records and employment outcomes. *N.Y.U. Review of Law and Social Change, The Harbinger*, 41, 271–286. https://ssrn.com/abstract=2938768.

Leasure, P. (2019). Securing private housing with a criminal record. *Journal of Offender Rehabilitation*, 58(1), 30–49. https://doi.org/10.1080/10509674.2018.1549182

Leasure, P., & Kaminski, R. (2021). The impact of a multiple conviction record on hiring outcomes. *Crime & Delinquency*, 67(6–7), 1022–1045. https://doi.org/10.1177/0011128720973150

LeBel, T. P. (2008). 'Perceptions of and responses to stigma', *Sociology Compass*, 2(3), 409–32. http://doi.org/10.1111/j.1751-9020.2007.00081.x

LeBel, T. P. (2012), Invisible Stripes? Formerly Incarcerated Persons' Perceptions Of Stigma. *Deviant Behavior*, 33(2), 89–107. DOI: 10.1080/01639625.2010.538365

Li, E. (2023). The Qianke system in China: Disorganisation, discrimination and dispersion. *Criminology & Criminal Justice*, 23(4), 568-587. https://doi.org/10.1177/17488958231161436

Link, B. G. & Phelan, J. (2014). Stigma power. *Social Sciences and Medicine*, 103, 24-32. https://doi.org/10.1016/j.socscimed.2013.07.035

Link, B. G. & Phelan, J. C. (2001). Conceptualizing stigma. *Annual Review of Sociology*, 27, 363–385. https://doi.org/10.1146/annurev.soc.27.1.363

Link, B. G., Yang, L. H., Phelan, J. C., & Collins, P. Y. (2004). Measuring mental illness stigma. *Schizophrenia Bulletin*, 30(3), 511–541. doi:10.1093/oxfordjournals.schbul.a007098

Livingstone, C. & Rintoul, A. (2021). Gambling-related suicidality: stigma, shame, and neglect. *The Lancet Public Health*, 6(1), e4 –e5.

Livingston, J. D., Milne, T., Fang, M. L., & Amari, E. (2012). The effectiveness of interventions for reducing stigma related to substance use disorders: A systematic review. *Addiction*, 107(1), 39–50. https://doi.org/10.1111/j.1360-0443.2011.03601.x

Luberto, C. M., Hyland, K. A., Streck, J. M., Temel, B., & Park, E. R. (2016). Stigmatic and sympathetic attitudes toward cancer patients who smoke: A qualitative analysis of an online discussion board forum. *Nicotine & Tobacco Research*, 18(12), 2194–2201. https://doi.org/10.1093/ntr/ntw166

Lucken, K., & Brancale, J. (2023). Getting down to work: The employment attitudes of persons with a felony conviction and their behavioral implications. *Journal of Crime & Justice*, 46(5), 647–665. https://doi.org/10.1080/0735648X.2023.2231421

Luoma, J. B. (2011). Substance use stigma as a barrier to treatment and recovery. In Johnson, B. A. (Ed.), *Addiction Medicine*. Berlin: Springer, 1195–1216.

Luoma, J. B., Twohig, M. P., Waltz, T., Hayes, S. C., Roget, N., Padilla, M., & Fisher, G. (2007). An investigation of stigma in individuals receiving treatment for substance abuse. *Addictive Behaviors*, 32(7), 1331–1346. https://doi.org/10.1016/j.addbeh.2006.09.008

Lussier, P., McCuish, E., & Corrado, R. R. (2015). The adolescence–adulthood transition and desistance from crime: Examining the underlying structure of desistance. *Journal of Developmental and Life-Course Criminology*, 1(2), 87-117. https://doi.org/ 10.1007 /s40865-015-0007-0

Martin, K., Taylor, A., Howell, B., & Fox, A. (2020). Does criminal justice stigma affect health and health care utilization? A systematic review of public health and medical literature. *International Journal of Prisoner Health*, 16(3), 263–279. https://doi.org/10.1108/IJPH-01-2020-0005

Maruna, S. (2012). Elements of successful desistance signaling. *Criminology and Public Policy*, 11(1), 73–85. https://doi.org/10.1111/j.1745-9133.2012.00789.x

Masson, I. & Österman, L. (2017). Working with female offenders in restorative justice frameworks: Effective and ethical practice. *Probation Journal*, 64(4), 354–371. https://doi.org/10.1177/02645505177287

McCormick, A. V., Millar, H. A., & Paddock, G. B. (2014). *In the best interests of the child*. Abbotsford: Centre for Safer Schools and Communities, University of the Fraser Valley.

McGrath, J., Crossley, S., Lussier, M., Forster, N. (2023). Social capital and women's narratives of homelessness and multiple exclusion in northern England. *In-*

ternational Journal for Equity and Health, 22, 41. https://doi.org/10.1186/s12939-023-01846-1

McKenzie, S. K., Oliffe, J. L., Black, A., & Collings, S. (2022). Men's experiences of mental illness stigma across the lifespan: A scoping review. *American Journal of Men's Health*, 16(1), 1–16. https://doi.org/10.1177/15579883221074789

McNeill, F. & Maruna, S. (2007). Giving Up and Giving Back: Desistance, Generativity and Social Work with Offenders, in G. McIvor and P. Raynor (Eds.), *Developments in Work With Offenders*, Routledge, 224–239.

McWilliams, E., & Hunter, B. (2021). The impact of criminal record stigma on quality of life: A test of theoretical pathways. *American Journal of Community Psychology*, 67(1/2), 89–102. https://doi.org/10.1002/ajcp.12454

McWilliams, E., Stidham, J., & Hunter, B. (2022). Discrimination, social support, and health-related quality of life among individuals with criminal records. *Journal of Community Psychology*, 50(7), 3237–3251. https://doi.org/10.1002/jcop.22835

Meade, R. R. (2021). Territorial stigmatization in theory and practice, and its implications for community development. *Community Development Journal*, 56(2). 191–202. https://doi.org/10.1093/cdj/bsab002

Mejia-Lancheros, C., Lachaud, J., Woodhall-Melnik, J., O'Campo, P., Hwang, S. W., & Stergiopoulos, V. (2021). Longitudinal interrelationships of mental health discrimination and stigma with housing and well-being outcomes in adults with mental illness and recent experience of homelessness. *Social Science & Medicine*, 268. https://doi.org/10.1016/j.socscimed.2020.113463

Milton, D. E. M. (2012). On the ontological status of autism: The 'double empathy problem'. *Disability and Society*, 27(6), 883-887. https://doi.org/10.1080/09687599.2012.710008

Mimoun, E., & Margalit, D. (2023). Disclosing an invisible disability during a romantic relationship: Schizophrenia and epilepsy. *Sexuality & Disability*, 41(1), 63–80. https://doi.org/10.1007/s11195-023-09774-2

Mitchell, S. (2024). Relational trauma: the impact on family relationships of maternal imprisonment. *Families, Relationships and Societies* (online ahead of print). https://doi.org/10.1332/20467435Y2024D000000039

Mittal, D., Sullivan, G., Chekuri, L., Allee, E., & Corrigan, P. W. (2012). Empirical studies of self-stigma reduction strategies: A critical review of the literature. *Psychiatric Services*, 63(10), 974–981. https://doi.org/10.1176/appi.ps.201100459

Moore, K. E., Stuewig, J. B., & Tangney, J. P. (2013). Jail inmates' perceived and anticipated stigma: Implications for post-release functioning. *Self and Identity*. 12(5), 527–547. https://doi.org/10.1080/15298868.2012.702425

Moore, K. E., Stuewig, J. B., & Tangney, J. P. (2016). The effect of stigma on criminal offenders' functioning: A longitudinal mediational model. *Deviant Behavior*, 37(2), 196-218. https://doj.org/10.1080/01639625.2014.1004035

Moore, K., & Tangney, J. (2017). Managing the Concealable Stigma of Criminal Justice System Involvement: A Longitudinal Examination of Anticipated Stigma, Social Withdrawal, and Post-Release Adjustment. *Journal of Social Issues*, 73(2), 322–340. https://doi.org/10.1111/josi.12219

Moore, K., Milam, K., Folk, J., & Tangney, J. (2018). Self-stigma among criminal offenders: Risk and protective factors. *Stigma and Health*, 3(3), 241–252. https://doi.org/10.1037/sah0000092

Moore, K., Tangney, J., & Stuewig, J. (2016). The self-stigma process in criminal offenders. *Stigma and Health*, 1(3), 206–224. https://doi.org/10.1037/sah0000024

Moran, D. (2012). Prisoner reintegration and the stigma of prison time inscribed on the body. *Punishment and Society*, 14(5), 564-583. https://doi.org/10.1177/14624745124640

Morris, L. (2018). Haunted futures: The stigma of being a mother living apart from her child(ren) as a result of court-ordered court removal. *Sociological Review*, 66(4), 816-831. https://doi.org/10.1177/0038026118777448

Mueller A. K., Fuermaier A. B., Koerts J., & Tucha L. (2012). Stigma in attention deficit hyperactivity disorder. *Attention Deficit and Hyperactivity Disorders*, 4(3), 101–114. https://doi.org/10.1007/s12402-012-0085-3

Mueller, T. S. (2021). Blame, then shame? Psychological predictors in cancel culture behavior. *The Social Science Journal*, 1–14. https://doi.org/10.1080/03623319.2021.1949552

Murray, C. E., Crowe, A., & Brinkley, J. (2015). The stigma surrounding intimate partner violence: A cluster analysis study. *Partner Abuse*, 6(3), 320–336. https://doi.org/10.1891/1946-6560.6.3.320.

Murray, C. E., Crowe, A., & Overstreet, N. M. (2018) Sources and components of stigma experienced by survivors of intimate partner violence. *Journal of Interpersonal Violence*, 33(3),515-536. https://doi.org/10.1177/0886260515609565.

Neff, K. (2003). Self-compassion: An alternative conceptualization of a healthy attitude toward oneself. *Self and Identity*, 2(2), 85–101. https://doi.org/10.1080/15298860309032

Novac, S., Hermer, J., Paradis, E., & Kellen, A. (2006). *Justice and injustice: Homelessness, crime, victimization, and the criminal justice system*. Toronto: Centre for Urban and Community Studies, University of Toronto, and the John Howard Society of Toronto.

Nugent, B. & Schinkel, M. (2016). The Pains of Desistance. *Criminology & Criminal Justice*, 16(5), 568–84. https://doi.org/10.1177/1748895816634812

O'Connor, L. K., Yanos, P. T., & Firmin, R. L. (2018). Correlates and moderators of stigma resistance among people with severe mental illness. *Psychiatry Research*, 270, 198–204. https://doi.org/10.1016/j.psychres.2018.09.040

O'Donnell. A. T., Corrigan, F., & Gallagher, S. (2015). The impact of anticipated stigma on psychological and physical health problems in the unemployed group. *Frontiers in Psychology*, 6, 1263 https://doi.org/10.3389/fpsyg.2015.01263

Oga, E. A., Kraemer, J., Stewart, C., Mbote, D., Njuguna, S., Stockton, M., & Nyblade, L. (2020). Experienced sex-work stigma in male and female sex workers in Kenya: Development and validation of a scale. *Stigma and Health*, 5(3), 342–350. https://doi.org/10.1037/sah0000205

Omerov, P., Craftman, Å. G., Mattsson. E., & Klarare, A. (2020). Homeless persons' experiences of health and social care: A systematic integrative review. *Health and Social Care in the Community*, 28(1), 1-11. https://doi.org/10.1111/hsc.12857.

Oselin, S. S, Ross, J. G. M., Wang, Q. & Kang, W. (2024). Fair Chance Act failures? Employers' hiring of people with criminal records. *Criminology & Public Policy*, 23(2), 361–390.

Östman, M. & Kjellin, L. (2002). Stigma by association: Psychological factors in relatives of people with mental illness. *British Journal of Psychiatry*, 181(6), 494-498. https://doi.org/10.1192/bjp.181.6.494

Overstreet, N. M., & Quinn, D. M. (2013). The intimate partner violence stigmatization model and barriers to help seeking. *Basic and Applied Social Psychology*, 35(1), 109–122. doi:10.1080/01973533.2012.746599.

Overstreet, N. M., Gaskins, J. L., Quinn, D. M., & Williams, M.K. (2017). The moderating role of centrality on the association between internalized intimate partner violence-related stigma and concealment of physical IPV. *Journal of Social Issues*, 73 (2), 307-321.

Pager, D. (2003). The mark of a criminal record. *American Journal of Sociology*, 108(5), 937–975. https://doi.org/10. 1086/374403

Pager, D., Bonikowski, B., & Western, B. (2009). Discrimination in a low-wage labor market: A field experiment. *American Sociological Review*, 74(5), 777–799.

Pahwa, R., Fulginiti, A., Brekke, J.S., & Rice, E. (2017). Mental illness disclosure decision making. *American Journal of Orthopsychiatry*, 87(5), 575–584. https://doi.org/ 10. 1037/ ort00 00250.

Paquette, C. E., Syvertsen, J. L., & Pollini, R. A. (2018). Stigma at every turn: Health services experiences among people who inject drugs. *The International Journal on Drug Policy*, 57: 104–110. https://doi.org/10.1016/j.drugpo.2018.04.004

Paris, R., Herriott, A. L., Maru, M., Hacking, S. A., & Sommer, A. R. (2020). Secrecy versus disclosure: Women with substance use disorders share experiences in help seeking during pregnancy. *Maternal and Child Health Journal*, 24(11), 1396–1403. https://doi.org/10.1007/s10995-020-03006-1

Pattyn, E., Verhaeghe, M. & Bracke, P. (2015). The gender gap in mental health service use. *Social Psychiatry and Psychiatric Epidemiology*, 50, 1089–1095. https://doi.org/10.1007/s00127-015-1038-x

Pryor, J. B., Reeder, G. D., & Monroe, A. E. (2012). The infection of bad company: Stigma by association. *Journal of Personality and Social Psychology*, 102(2), 224–241. https://doi.org/10.1037/a0026270

Qiu, L., Feng, Y., Luo, J., Zhang, Y., & Yang, Q. (2022). Predictors of personal depression stigma in medical students in China: differences in male and female groups. *Medical Education Online*, 27(1), 1–8. https://doi.org/10.1080/10872981.2022.2093427

Quinn, D. M., & Chaudoir, S. R. (2009). Living with a concealable stigmatized identity: The impact of anticipated stigma, centrality, salience, and cultural stigma on psychological distress and health. *Journal of Personality and Social Psychology*, 97(4), 634–651. https://doi.org/10.1037/a0015815

Quinn, D. M., & Earnshaw, V. A. (2011). Understanding concealable stigmatized identities: The role of identity in psychological, physical, and behavioral outcomes. *Social Issues and Policy Review*, 5(1), 160–190. https://doi.org/10.1111/j.1751-2409.2011.01029.x.

Quinn, D. M. & Earnshaw, V. A. (2013). Concealable stigmatized identities and psychological well-being. *Social and Personality Psychology Compass* 7(1), 40–51. https://doi.org/10.1111/SPC3.12005

Ramakers, A. (2022). Secrecy as best policy? Stigma management and employment outcomes after release from prison. *British Journal of Criminology*, 62(2), 501–518. https://doi.org/10.1093/bjc/azab068

Rayson, J. & Alba, B. (2019). Experiences of stigma and discrimination as predictors of mental health help-seeking among sex workers. *Sexual Relationship Therapy*, 34(3), 277–289. https://doi.org/10.1080/14681994.2019.1628488

Rea, Jessica (2023). Social relationships, stigma, and wellbeing through experiences of homelessness in the United Kingdom, *Social Issues*, 79(1), 465-493. https://doi.org/10.1111/josi.12572.

Redmond, N., Aminawung, J., Morse, D., Zaller, N., Shavit, S., & Wang, E. (2020). Perceived discrimination based on criminal record in healthcare settings and self-reported health status among formerly incarcerated individuals. *Journal of Urban Health*, 97(1), 105–111. https://doi.org/10.1007/s11524-019-00382-0

Reilley, J., Ho, I., & Williamson, A. (2022). A systematic review of the effect of stigma on the health of people experiencing homelessness. *Health and Social Care in the Community*, 30(6), 2128-2141. https://doi.org/10.1111/hsc.13884.

Ricciardelli, R. & Mooney, T. (2018). The decision to disclose: Employment after prison." *Journal of Offender Rehabilitation*, 57(6), 343–366.

Rima, D., Akbolatova, M., Orynbasar, T., Arailym, J., & Beaver, K. (2023). Long-term health and economic consequences associated with being processed through the criminal justice system for males. *American Journal of Criminal Justice*, 48(5), 1063–1079. https://doi.org/10.1007/s12103-022-09723-3

Robinson, K.M., Robinson, K.A., Scherer, A.M. and Mackin, M.L. (2024), Patient Perceptions of Weight Stigma Experiences in Healthcare: A Qualitative Analysis. *Health Expectations*, 27(3), e70013. https://doi.org/10.1111/hex.70013

Roebuck, B. (2008). Homelessness, victimization, and crime: Knowledge and actionable recommendations. Public Safety Canada. https://www.publicsafety.gc.ca/lbrr/archives/cnmcs-plcng/cn35305-eng.pdf

Rovira, M. (2024). Invisible stripes? A field experiment on the disclosure of a criminal record in the British labour market and the potential effects of introducing ban-the-box policies. *The British Journal of Criminology*, 64(4), 827–845. https://doi.org/10.1093/bjc/azad063

Rüsch N., Angermeyer, M. C., & Corrigan, P. W. (2005). Mental illness stigma: Concepts, consequences, and initiatives to reduce stigma. *European Psychiatry*. 20(8), 529–539. https://doi.org/10.1016/j.eurpsy.2005.04.004

Rutter, N. and Barr, U. (2011). Being a good woman: Stigma, relationships and desistance. *Probation Journal*, 68(2), 166–185. https://doi.org/10.1177/02645505211010336

Ryan, L., Quigley, F., Birney, S., Crotty, M., Conlan, O. and Walsh, J.C. (2024), 'Beyond the scale': A qualitative exploration of the impact of weight stigma experienced by patients with obesity in general practice. *Health Expectations*, 27: e14098. https://doi.org/10.1111/hex.14098

Sallmann, J. (2010). Living with stigma: Women's experiences of prostitution and substance use. *Affilia: Journal of Women and Social Work*, 25(2), 146–159. https://doi.org/10.1177/0886109910364362.

Sánchez, F. J. (2023). Self-compassion in today's regressive sociopolitical climate. *Clinical Psychology: Science and Practice*, 30(1), 43–44. https://doi.org/10.1037/cps0000115

Santos, M. R., Jaynes, C. M., & Thomas, D. M. (2023). How to overcome the cost of a criminal record for getting hired. *Criminology*, 61(3), 582–621. https://doi.org/10.1111/1745-9125.12345

Sattler, K. M., Deane, F. P., Tapsell, L., & Kelly, P. J. (2018). Gender differences in the relationship of weight-based stigmatisation with motivation to exercise and physical activity in overweight individuals. *Health Psychology Open*, 5(1), 1–11. https://doi.org/10.1177/2055102918759691

Sayed, T. A., Ali, M. M., & Hadad, S. (2021). Risk factors and impact of stigma on psychiatric patients in Sohag. *The Egyptian Journal of Neurology, Psychiatry and Neurosurgery*, 57, Article 148, 1-8. https://doi.org/10.1186/s41983-021-00403-3

Scambler, G. (2007). Sex work stigma: Opportunistic migrants in London. *Sociology*, 41(6), 1079–1096. https://doi.org/10.1177/0038038507082316

Scharff-Smith, P. (2014). *When the innocents are punished: The children of imprisoned parents*. New York: Palgrave Macmillan.

Schneider, V. (2018). The prison to homelessness pipeline: Criminal record checks, race, and disparate impact. *Indiana Law Journal*, 93(2). 923–947. https://www.repository.law.indiana.edu/ilj/vol93/iss2/4

Schneider, V. (2019). Racism knocking at the door: The use of criminal background checks in rental housing. *University of Richmond Law Review*, 53(3), 923–947.

Schwarz, C. (2020). Transitioning house: A "safe umbrella" from criminal stigmatization? *Journal of Offender Rehabilitation*, 59(5), 285–314. https://doi.org/10.1080/10509674.2020.1745978

Selbin, J., McCrary, J., & Epstein, J. (2018). Unmarked? Criminal record clearing and employment outcomes. *The Journal of Criminal Law and Criminology*, 108(1), 1–72.

Sharpe, G. (2015). Precarious Identities: "young" motherhood, desistance and stigma. *Criminology and Criminal Justice*, 15(4), 407-422. https://doi.org/10.1177/1748895815572163

Sharpe, G. (2024). *Women, stigma, and desistance from crime: Precarious identities in the transition to adulthood*. London: Routledge.

Shaw, M. (2023). Financial strain, the transference of stigma, and residential instability: A qualitative analysis of the long-term effects of parental incarceration. *Family Relations*, 72(4), 1773–1789. https://doi.org/10.1111/fare.12763

Sheppard, A. & Ricciardelli. R. (2020). Employment after prison: Navigating conditions of precarity and stigma. *European Journal of Probation*, 12(1), 34–52. https://doi.org/10.1177/206622032090825

Siegel, K., Lune, H., & Meyer, I. H. (1998). Stigma management among gay/bisexual men with HIV/AIDS. *Qualitative Sociology*, 21(1), 3 –23. https://doi.org/10.1023/A:1022102825016

Sinko, R., DeAngelis, T., Alpajora, B., Beker, J., & Kramer, I. (2020). Experience of stigma post incarceration: A qualitative study. *The Open Journal of Occupational Therapy*, 8(3), 1–16. https://doi.org/10.15453/2168-6408.1610

Smith, S., & Broege, N. (2020). Searching for work with a criminal record. *Social Problems*, 67(2), 208–232. https://doi.org/10.1093/socpro/spz009

Stewart, R., & Uggen, C. (2020). Criminal records and college admissions: A modified experimental audit. *Criminology*, 58(1), 156–188. https://doi.org/10.1111/1745-9125.12229

Stewart, R., Wright, B., Smith, L., Steven Roberts, S., Russell, N. (2021). Gendered stereotypes and norms: A systematic review of interventions designed to shift attitudes and behaviour. *Heliyon*, 7(4), e06660. https://doi.org/10.1016/j.heliyon.2021.e06660

Stone, R. (2015). Pregnant women and substance use: Fear, stigma, and barriers to care. *Health and Justice*, 3(2). 3-15. 10.1186/s40352-015-0015-5

Stone, R. (2016). 'Desistance and Identity Repair: Redemption Narratives as Resistance to Stigma', *British Journal of Criminology,* 56(5), 956–75. https://doi.org/10.1093/bjc/azv081

Stone, R., Morash, M., Goodson, M., Smith, S., & Cobbina, J. (2018). Women on Parole, Identity Processes, and Primary Desistance. *Feminist Criminology,* 13(4), 382–403. DOI: 10.1177/1557085116670004

Sundaresh, R., Yi, Y., Roy, B., Riley, C., Wildeman, C., & Wang, E. (2020). Exposure to the US criminal legal system and well-being: A 2018 cross-sectional study. *American Journal of Public Health,* 110, S116–S122. https://doi.org/10.2105/AJPH.2019.305414

Sylaska, K. M., & Edwards, K. M. (2014). Disclosure of intimate partner violence to informal social support network members: A review of the literature. *Trauma, Violence, & Abuse,* 15(1), 3–21. https://doi.org/10.1177/1524838013496335.

Tally, A. E. & Littlefield, A. (2014). Pathways between concealable stigmatized identities and substance misuse. *Social and Personality Psychology Compass,* 8(10), 569–582. https://doi-org/10.1111/spc3.12117

Taylor, M. & Spang, T. (2017). "I'd prefer an applicant who doesn't have a delinquency history": Delinquents in the labor market." *Journal of Juvenile Justice,* 6(1), 67–81.

Tilghman-Osborne, C., Cole, D. A., Felton, J. W., & Ciesla, J. A. (2008). Relation of guilt, shame, behavioral and characterological self-blame to depressive symptoms in adolescents over time. *Journal of Social and Clinical Psychology,* 27(8), 809–842. https://doi.org/10.1521/jscp.2008.27.8.809

Timko, C., Schultz, N. R., Britt, J., & Cucciare, M. A. (2016). Transitioning from detoxification to substance use disorder treatment: Facilitators and barriers. *Journal of Substance Abuse Treatment,* 70, 64–72. https://doi.org/10.1016/j.jsat.2016.07.010

Tinney, E. (2024). The "STICKINESS" of stigma: Guilt by association after a friend's arrest. *Criminology,* 61(4); 354-393. https://doi.org/10.1111/1745-9125.12333

Tovey, L., Winder, B., & Blagden, N. (2023). "It's ok if you were in for robbery or murder, but sex offending, that's a no no": a qualitative analysis of the experiences of 12 men with sexual convictions seeking employment. *Psychology, Crime & Law,* 29(6), 653–676. https://doi.org/10.1080/1068316X.2022.2030736

Treloar, C., Stardust, Z., Cama, E., & Kim, J. (2021). Rethinking the relationship between sex work, mental health and stigma: a qualitative study of sex workers in Australia, *Social Science and Medicine,* 113468. https://doi.org/10.1016/j.socscimed.2020.113468

Turan, J. M., et al. (2019). Challenges and Opportunities in Examining and Addressing Intersectional Stigma and Health. *BMC Medicine,* 17 (7).

Tyler, I., & Slater, T. (2018). Rethinking the sociology of stigma. *The Sociological Review,* 66(4), 721-743. https://doi.org/10.1177/0038026118777425

Uggen, C. Vuolo, M., Lageson, S., Ruhland, E., & Whitham, H. K. (2014). The edge of stigma: An experimental audit of the effects of low-level criminal records on employment. *Criminology*, 52(4), 627–654. https://doi.org/10.1111/1745-9125.12051

Van Boekel, L. C., et al., (2013). Stigma among health professionals towards patients with substance use disorders and its consequences for healthcare delivery: Systematic review. *Drug and Alcohol Dependence*, 131(1–2), 23-35, https://doi.org/10.1016/j.drugalcdep.2013.02.018

van den Berg, C. J. W, Blommaert, L., Bijleveld, C., & Ruiter, S. (2020). Employment opportunities for ex-offenders: A field experiment on how type of crime and applicants' ethnic background affect employment opportunities for low-educated men in the Netherlands. *Research in Social Stratification and Mobility*, 65, 100476. https://doi.org/10.1016/j.rssm.2020.100476

van der Sanden, R. L. M., Bos, A. E. R., Stutterheim, S. E., Pryor, J. B., and Kok, G. (2015). Stigma by Association Among Family Members of People with a Mental Illness: A Qualitative Analysis. *Journal of Community and Applied Social Psychology*, 25(5), 400–417. https://doi.org/10.1002/casp.2221

Visser, M. J., Peters, R. M., & Luman, M. (2024). Understanding ADHD-related stigma: A gender analysis of young adult and key stakeholder perspectives. *Neurodiversity*, 2. https://doi.org/10.1177/27546330241274664

Wacquant, L. (2007). Territorial stigmatization in the age of advanced marginality. *Thesis Eleven*, 91(1), 66–77. https://doi.org/10.1177/0725513607082003

Wahto, R. & Swift J. (2016). Labels, Gender-Role Conflict, Stigma, and Attitudes Toward Seeking Psychological Help in Men. *American Journal of Men's Health*, 10(3),181-191. doi:10.1177/1557988314561491

Weitzer, R. (2018). Resistance to sex work stigma, *Sexualities*, 21(5–6), 717–729. https://doi.org/10.1177/1363460716684

Winnick, T. & Bodkin, M. (2008). Anticipated stigma and stigma management among those to be labeled "ex-con." *Deviant Behavior*, 29: 295–333. https://doi.org/10.1080/01639620701588081.

Wong, C. W., Holroyd, E. & Bingham, A. (2011). Stigma and sex work from the Perspective of Female sex Workers in Hong Kong. *Sociology of Health and Illness*, 33 (1): 50-65.

Wu, L-T., Blazer, D. G., Li, T., & Woody, G. E. (2011). Treatment use and barriers among adolescents with prescription opioid use disorders. *Addictive Behaviors*, 36(12), 1233–1239. https://doi.org/10.1016/j.addbeh.2011.07.033

Xiao, Z., Li, X., Qiao, S., Zhou, Y., & Shen, Z. (2018). Coping, social support, stigma, and gender difference among people living with HIV in Guangxi, China. *Psychology, Health & Medicine*, 23(1), 18–29. https://doi.org/10.1080/13548506.2017.1300671

Yip, C. C. H., Fung, W. T. W., Leung, D. C. K., & Chan, K. K. S. (2023). The impact of stigma on engaged living and life satisfaction among people with mental illness in Hong Kong. *Quality of Life Research*, 32(1), 161–170. https://doi.org/10.1007/s11136-022-03218-8

Yin, M., Li, Z. and Zhou, C. (2020), Experience of stigma among family members of people with severe mental illness: A qualitative systematic review. *International Journal of Mental Health Nursing*, 29(2), 141-160. https://doi.org/10.1111/inm.12668

Youngren, W. A., Bishop, T., Carr, M., Mattera, E., & Pigeon, W. (2024). Nightmare types and suicide. *Dreaming*, 34(1), 1–7. https://doi.org/10.1037/drm0000261

Yu, B. C. L., Chio, F. H. N., Mak, W. W. S., Corrigan, P. W., & Chan, K. K. Y. (2021). Internalization process of stigma of people with mental illness across cultures: A meta-analytic structural equation modeling approach. *Clinical Psychology Review*, 87. https://doi.org/10.1016/j.cpr.2021.102029

Terms and Definitions

Anticipated stigma: An expectation or fear of experiencing enacted stigma.

Associative stigma (or courtesy stigma): The result of a process through which relatives or associates of stigmatized persons are discredited and stigmatized.

Compounded Stigma (or intersectional stigma): The convergence of multiple stigmatized identities within a person or group and resulting need to address their joint or compounded effects on health and wellbeing.

Concealable stigma: A stigma associated with signs or characteristics that are not apparent or readily discernable.

Disidentifiers: Various behavioural signs or signals meant to help dissociate oneself from a potentially spoiled identity.

Enacted stigma: A manifestation of public stigma through actions, inactions and intentions to act targeting the stigmatized group.

Intergenerational stigma: The experience of stigma by children because of their parents' conduct or condition.

Masking (or camouflaging): The efforts made by an individual to hide or supress symptoms, behaviours, and difficulties they are experiencing, often in anticipation of stigma.

Ostracization: Excluding someone from society, groups, friendship, conversation, or privileges, often by general and often tacit consent.

Perceived stigma: People's perception that they or others like them are being stigmatized.

Public stigma: Public attitudes, implicit or explicit, towards a stigmatized group, or how the public or a community views a stigmatized group.

Redemption script: A narrative to redeem oneself of one's past and assert a meaningful future.

Resilience: The maintenance of positive adaptation by individuals despite experiences of significant adversity.

Resilience: The process and outcome of successfully adapting to difficult or challenging life experiences, especially through mental, emotional, and behavioral flexibility and adjustment to external and internal demands.

Self-stigma (or internalized stigma): A situation in which someone identifies with a stigmatized group, accepts the negative judgment of others, and internalizes negative thoughts, feelings, and self-evaluations associated with the stigmatized identity.

Self-validation: A self-compassionate practice in which people are taught to consider and name the ways in which their emotions make sense.

Stigma power: Instances in which stigma processes achieve the aims of stigmatizers with respect to the exploitation, control or exclusion of others.

Stigma resistance: An ongoing, active process of using one's experiences, skills and knowledge to develop a positive identity.

Stigma: "The situation of the person who is disqualified from full social acceptance" (Goffman, 1963).

Stigma-informed approach: A stigma-informed approach is essentially about empowering people to cope with stigma in a healthy and self-empowering way and helping them develop resilience.

Territorial stigma: The negative social judgment attached to people living, working or frequenting certain places.

www.ingramcontent.com/pod-product-compliance
Lightning Source LLC
Chambersburg PA
CBHW071711020426
42333CB00017B/2222